THE
MENTAL
EDGE IN TRADING

THE
MENTAL
EDGE IN TRADING

*Adapt Your Personality Traits
and Control Your Emotions
to Make Smarter Investments*

JASON WILLIAMS, MD

**with Foreword and Commentary by
LARRY WILLIAMS**

New York   Chicago   San Francisco   Lisbon   London
Madrid   Mexico City   Milan   New Delhi   San Juan
Seoul   Singapore   Sydney   Toronto

1 2 3 4 5 6 7 8 9 0   DOC/DOC   1 8 7 6 5 4 3 2

ISBN: 978-0-07-179940-9
MHID: 0-07-179940-0

e-ISBN: 978-0-07-179941-6
e-MHID: 0-07-179941-9

This publication is designed to provide accurate and authoritative information in regard to the subject matter covered. It is sold with the understanding that neither the author nor the publisher is engaged in rendering legal, accounting, or other professional service. If legal advice or other expert assistance is required, the services of a competent professional person should be sought.

—From a Declaration of Principles Jointly Adopted by a Committee of the American Bar Association and a Committee of Publishers and Associations

McGraw-Hill books are available at special quantity discounts to use as premiums and sales promotions, or for use in corporate training programs. To contact a representative, please e-mail us at bulksales@mcgraw-hill.com.

This book is printed on acid-free paper.

To the three joys in my life: Richard, Violet, and Sylva.

I love you each infinitely.

CONTENTS

FOREWORD

As parents we like to think that our children will learn life's lessons from us. We don't often think we learn much from them; we've been there, done that. Our purpose is to break the ice, to show them the way. This book, by my son Dr. Jason Williams, turns that notion upside down for me.

While I have been trading the markets for some 50 years now, in this book I learned from my son. The child was the teacher. The first thing I learned is that in order to change taking incorrect action and not changing detrimental habits, we really do need to know ourselves.

Without knowing yourself, how can change occur?

I kind of thought I knew most of the things about the market as well as my own personality as a trader. I was flat out wrong. When I took the personality profile test that Jason gave me, I immediately learned my strengths and weaknesses. What surprised me was that I had never realized any of these points before.

I always knew I could develop great mechanical trading systems, but could never figure out why I had such a hard time trading or following them myself. My best trading has almost always come from a much more freestyle form of trading, something that can't be bottled up or reduced to a single mathematical formula. It was not until I took the personality test that I understood why I can develop good systems but simply had problems following them.

What I found was that the shoe didn't fit. While intellectually I can develop systems, my personality is not one to follow them. That was a real breakthrough for me as it crystallized the best possible trading strategy for me. I was able to find the shoe that fits. That realization, as to how I function as a trader, also taught me how I can best use mechanical trading systems. This was a double win for me; I learned my best personal trading strategy as well as how to best use trading systems!

When they were shown to me, that was very much an "A-ha!" experience. I instinctively and intuitively knew those were the areas that made me a good trader as well as the areas I needed to work on.

Risk has never bothered me, so I have not been afraid to take trades. The test confirmed that. What I didn't know was that my largest trading weaknesses have been my lack of paying attention to detail. Clearly I'm not the world's best detail person, not even close, but I never realized until reading Jason's work and understanding my personality how much of a hindrance that was to making my trading even more successful.

It is my hope, and Jason's, that as you read this book, you will have deep insights into your personality. That can be accomplished by simply looking over the shoulders of the personalities of some phenomenal traders.

In reading this book, I picked up additional insights into successful trading, thanks to the wonderful people who facilitated Jason's work. My hat goes off to these individual traders, who opened the doors of their hearts and souls so mere mortals like us will become better at this business of trading and investing.

We typically read books on trading and investing to learn about the market. That's not true of this book. In this book you will learn about yourself . . . you will learn how successful traders think and respond and be given techniques you can use to improve the way you go about trading.

That's what is terribly unique about this book. It was written specifically for you. The data in this book are presented specifically to make you a better trader.

If you know the enemy and you know yourself, your victory will not be in doubt.

You have known the enemy; now you can know yourself.

Larry Williams
Trader and proud father
St. Croix, U.S. Virgin Islands
2012

Imagine there were a way to assess and measure your innate personality traits . . . with incredible detail and scientific validity. Then imagine there were a body of research data that could help you make sense of your specific personality traits . . . and better yet, teach you how to apply your own cluster of personality traits to become a better, wiser, and more consistently profitable market trader.

Well, there is. And I want to tell you about it!

My name is Jason Williams. I am a medical doctor and adult psychiatrist who trained at what is often considered the nation's (if not the world's) preeminent hospital and medical center: Johns Hopkins, in Baltimore, Maryland. I am also the son of Larry Williams, whom many consider to be one of the world's most eminent futures/commodities traders. (He is also a pretty good dad.)

For some time, my father and I have mused over, discussed, and debated how human emotions and the personality traits behind them relate to someone becoming a successful, or unsuccessful, market speculator. It is one of our favorite topics of conversation, and given our respective backgrounds, it probably makes sense that this particular fascination moved us to learn more and then write a book about it.

Not only did we dig deeply into the scientific literature on this subject, but we also started compiling some data of our own! Starting in 2010, we began giving a standardized personality test (the NEO PI-R) to a group of hand-picked, top-notch market traders (all people personally known to be very active traders and to have successfully traded the markets with consistency, year after year, many even for decades). We then discussed their results with them individually, to get a deeper appreciation of what makes a great trader. This book contains our findings.

Rest assured, this is not some pie-in-the-sky, nonsensical psychobabble or flim-flam that can't hold water. Nor is it your run-of-the-mill motivational self-help material written by people who need even more help than you do! Nor is it some brief and diluted personality quiz (and trust me, those are out there on the Internet, and they're worth exactly what they cost . . . zilch) that leaves you with only vague generalizations and nothing new or concrete to approach the markets with.

Rather, the book in your hands is something much more valuable and much more real. All of the principals contained within these pages are based on hard science and our current understanding of the human brain and mental life (psychology). As far as we are aware, this is the first treatise that seriously and in great depth explores the link between successful trading and personality traits.

Look, it's no great secret that managing one's emotions is *huge* when it comes to surviving the turbulent ups and downs of the markets. It can be a pretty wild ride, and all along the way we are each emotionally moved by, and respond to the markets' activity, based on who we are as unique individuals. If you deny that your emotions are just as vital as your favorite trading system or market indicator, you are either in a state of denial or merely a "paper trader."

The reality is that classical finance theory, as taught in universities, does not take into account the raw human emotions involved in decision making. Classical finance assumes that we all act as rational beings, when in fact we all know that we don't. The decisions of investors and traders are shaped by not only sound logic, but also by emotions within a personal life context. We are unavoidably prone to such psychological biases when it comes to trading the markets. Understanding our own personalities and temperaments, and even more so how they shape our financial decision making, is a fundamentally crucial task for any investors hoping to achieve good returns. It can be quite daunting to think about how the numerous personality and emotional variables can interfere with implementing and sticking to your trading strategy. This book sets out in a very systematic way how to approach your personality and its influence on your trading, and how to master them.

There is no mistaking it: our emotions are real. After all, this is real money. Real contracts for commodities, stocks, bonds, and currencies are on the line. Learning to understand and adapt to your emotional strengths and weaknesses is just as critical as any other aspect of your trading. Even the most seasoned traders still grapple with the emotional component of trading. One major hypothesis is that the successful trader has learned, one way or another, to adapt to his or her own blend of personality traits and, over time, has learned to conquer the emotional aspects of trading because of this healthy adaptation. We should all learn from these master traders!

The best way to read this book is to first go through it cover to cover, and then refer back to each section as needed during particular market conditions or personal contemplations. Although the real "meat and potatoes" of how personality relates to traders starts in Chapter 15, it really will be helpful to read the first 14 chapters on personality and the human mental life, in order to get a good, solid foundation under your feet. Also, as you read this book, pay special attention to the mental edge tips listed at the end of each chapter, as it is into these that we have distilled the most critical concepts! Finally, it is imperative that at some point you take the NEO PI-R, in order to measure your own personality traits and see how you stack up against the world at large and against the top traders in the world. By doing so, you will be well on the road to knowing how to adapt your own personality to prosperous trading. This test can be administered by any accredited psychologist or psychiatrist who is trained in giving, scoring, and interpreting it.

Our ultimate hope is that this treasure trove of knowledge will help you better understand yourself, how you currently trade, and how you can learn to trade more effectively. We would love to hear your comments!

Jason Williams, MD
emaildoctorj@yahoo.com

THE
MENTAL
EDGE IN TRADING

CHAPTER 1

The Human Mind: A Primer

Your entire mental life (the biosystem known as the human mind) is defined by and can be broken down into a combination of three basic elements:

1. Thoughts
2. Emotions
3. Behaviors

These three components are *not* discrete. That is, they do not have clear boundaries and, in fact, are inextricably related to one another. For example, your thoughts clearly affect the way you feel, and your feelings (urges) often drive your behaviors. Nevertheless, these three realms are sufficiently different to provide a commonsense distinction and framework for what constitutes human mental life. And we all know what they mean: we all talk in terms of thinking, feeling, and doing.

It is also important to observe how each of these three elements can (either for good or bad) drive or feed into one another in any direction, as depicted in Figure 1.1

As a very simple example, a negative thought ("How could I have made such a stupid mistake?") will tend to cause one to feel worse (low self-esteem, incompetence, worthlessness, demoralization, sadness, and so on), and such feelings can evolve into negative actions ("drinking my blues away"). But again, notice that the

Figure 1.1 The inextricable interactions of thoughts, actions, and feelings.

arrows point in both directions. By drinking your blues away, you may feel guilty, and so on.

One final point on the core constituents of the human mind: The term "subconscious" ("or subconscious mind") is often used in many different contexts, and it has no single or precise definition. Also, there is no reliable way to tap into the subconscious mind to find out what it is thinking or feeling. Anyone can claim to understand and interpret the subconscious, but there is no way to scientifically study or prove such claims at this time. All of this greatly limits the significance of the subconscious mind as a definition-bearing concept. As a consequence the term tends to be avoided in academic and scientific settings.

We should not go so far as to say that the subconscious has no meaning at all or that it doesn't exist. But for all intents and purposes, it does not come into play when trying to understand how the human mind interacts with market trading. So we will leave this concept alone for the rest of this book and instead focus on feelings, thoughts, and actions.

Mental Edge Tips
- Always strive to be aware of and in tune with your thoughts, emotions, and actions and how they are interrelating and driving one another at any given moment in time.
- Trying to understand your subconscious mind is like trying to chase the wind. Merely trying to master your conscious mind (thoughts, emotions, and behaviors) is a plenty difficult task in itself, and I suggest you start there!

CHAPTER 2

How Does the Brain
Generate the Mind?

How does the brain generate the mind? The answer is very simple: we do not know.

Since the time of Plato, philosophers and anatomists alike have debated and struggled to figure out how the human brain produces the mind (thoughts, feelings, and behaviors). Over the centuries, inquisitive and intrepid scientists pretty well figured out how all the other organs in the human body fit together and perform their respective jobs. For example, we know quite well the various components and mechanics that are at work inside a cardiac cell, and we have clear explanations as to how living heart tissue functions as a nice pump to move blood around the rest of the circulatory system. We also have a good grasp on the kidneys, bones, the pancreas, and so on. But the brain . . . ah, the brain is truly in a league all its own.

Today, despite multiple advances in the neurosciences (such as PET scans and other high-tech brain imaging modalities, an increasingly better understanding of neurons and neurotransmitters, and so on), the world's very best scientists still are quite puzzled by, and even largely clueless about, how the three-pound lump of tissue know as the brain generates thoughts, feelings, and actions. Sure, we know that the brain consists of neurons, and that these neurons are endowed with certain electrochemical properties. We know there are certain tracts and regions of the brain that are involved with different functions. But how human consciousness springs forth is truly one of the great mysteries of the universe. Perhaps on this plane we will never be able to figure out the connections between brain tissue and mental life, or perhaps one day we will. But for now, the answers to this "mind-brain problem" remain very much hidden from our own ability to understand them.

If people tell you otherwise, they clearly do not know what they are talking about.

Mental Edge Tips
- The mainframe computer warehoused inside your skull is the most powerful and fastest computer known to mankind and is the most intricate "thing" in the known universe. Think of it: All of the world's supercomputers were themselves designed and programmed by human minds. Marvel at the beauty and elegance of the human mind.
- Don't get bogged down in the philosophy of the brain and mind. Focus on the here and now!

CHAPTER 3

Anatomy of the Brain 101

Although we don't really know how the brain generates the mind, we do have a pretty good understanding of what different regions of the brain do and how they are connected to one another by various pathways.

Popular science will tell you that the major distinction inside your head is "right brain" versus "left brain." Please delete that thought from your memory banks. You will hear people say, "I am a right-brained person." Rubbish. Although the right and left sides of the brain have some differences, they actually have far more things in common. More important, the two sides of the brain are always working together. It's not like the right brain and left brain work independently. You only have one brain at work.

The way you really need to think about the brain's anatomy is in a hierarchical way: superficial brain (cortex) versus deep brain (subcortex). You are about to read a very gross oversimplification of the brain's architecture, but for your purposes (as a trader or investor), it's all you really need to know.

Some people like to think that trading is all about logic: analyzing all available data, considering the various pros and cons of different courses of action, and then coming to a logically sound conclusion. If only it were that simple!!

Sure, intellectually smarter people do, by and large, make for better traders. Sound logical reasoning is a valued asset for any trader. And the more practical wisdom you have gathered from real-world experiences over the years also helps. But clearly intelligence is not the whole picture.

In fact, there are plenty of very successful traders who sport very normal intelligence quotients (IQs). There have also been bloody geniuses who failed miserably trying to trade the markets. Take, for example, Sir Isaac Newton, the man who single-handedly solved the riddle of gravity and then went on to figure out the laws of motion for the entire universe. Were you aware that Newton (despite knowing so much about gravity, falls, and crashes) was wiped out by the 1720 stock market crash because his emotions got the best of him in a bubble market? Emotionally charged with excitement by a peaking market, Newton purchased stocks at precisely the wrong time.

Poor Newton. He fell for the same old temptation that to this day still propels many bright, but novice, investors and traders into ruin: enthusiastically buying at market peaks and selling in a panic, when it is too late and the market has already hit a new low. It's an emotional pattern as old and true as time itself. Logically, we all know to buy low and sell high. Emotionally, we often do the reverse.

Here is a great quote from Buck Rogers (the IBM Buck Rogers, not the science fiction one): "People buy emotionally, then justify with logic."

This quote gets to the fact that people all too frequently make purchasing (or investing) decisions based purely on emotions, with little logic behind them. They may well rationalize their decision afterwards by using logic, but the decision itself is often made on emotion, with logic only playing a *secondary* role.

Ask yourself this: The last time you bought a new gadget, let's say a mobile phone, did you choose the make and model based on an absolutely complete review and comparison of all the handsets available on the market? Did you really read, analyze, and do a side-by-side comparison of all the detailed specs, features, and prices of the phones there were to choose from?

Or did you only briefly look at the main specs and then buy the phone because it "looked cool" (a sleek design, a catchy marketing campaign, or perhaps it's the make that is all the rage right now)? Did you actually buy the phone based more on a "feeling" that it was the right one? Did you even buy it simply because you desired it?

They don't call it "buyer's remorse" for nothing! You make a purchase based on your feelings, but it's only after you get home and unpack your new phone that you realize there are a few short-comings to it . . . things that you did not know about, or even con-template, prior to the purchase. Maybe the speaker phone is not quite loud enough, and it turns out that it's the most important feature for your telephoning needs. Or maybe several days later you learn about a new phone model that is about to be released that is even more appealing and "cool" than the one you just bought. If only you had investigated a little more! And of course the store knows all about buyer's remorse. That's why it has a 15 percent restocking fee!

Oftentimes we don't realize that this process is happening in the moment, because rarely do we think long and hard about how deeply our emotions are influencing us. We just *feel* them.

Why does this happen? It's actually simple anatomy.

Like I said, our brains have two main parts: an outer shell and an inner core. The brain's shell is the cerebral cortex and is the outermost layer of the brain. The cortex near the front of the brain is the part we use purposefully, while other cortical areas are hard at work without our even being aware of them (receiv-ing, interpreting, and processing information). The core, on the other hand, is located underneath the shell; it is composed of the limbic system and amygdala and is often referred to as the subcortex.

The core of the brain is where emotions and memories are formed and kept, while the shell is where complex thoughts, deci-sions, and behaviors are orchestrated and initiated. See Figure 3.1.

The core is tucked away in the center of the brain and is pri-meval. It is where most of the basic and primitive mental functions reside—our sense of survival, fear, anger, hunger, sex drive, and so on. The core is primarily designed to makes decisions very quickly and in a very black and white manner. The core does not "think." It reacts!

What happens if you are walking along in the jungle and sud-denly you see a tiger step out from the brush? You flee as fast as you can, naturally. This decision to immediately flee is all related

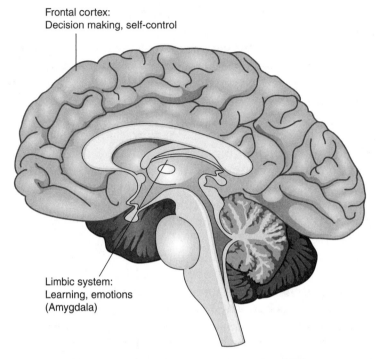

Figure 3.1 Basic brain anatomy: the core versus the shell.

to your brain's anatomy. Again, your memory (the last time I came across a tiger, it killed and ate my brother) and your feelings (I miss my brother) are located in your core, and it is your core that allows you to flee such a dangerous or hostile situation without giving it a second thought.

In evolutionary terms the cortex, or shell, is a much more recent development. The shell of our brains is also what separates us humans from other animals, including other primates. The shell is what gives humans intelligence and the spark of creativity. The cortex, especially in the frontal areas, is "the CEO of the brain": it plans, interprets, organizes, draws conclusions based on prior experiences, forms theories and hypotheses, weighs pros and cons, and makes decisions.

Another primary purpose of the shell is to regulate and modulate what the core is doing. For example, if the core tells us to be afraid because we hear a loud bang, the shell will analyze the situation and decide whether the bang is truly a danger that we should run away from, or if, instead, it is from a totally harmless source and can be filtered out and ignored, or even if the bang is actually a call of distress from somebody we love and who needs our urgent help, meaning we should actually be rushing *toward* the bang, not away from it!

There are two main brain pathways, or circuits, that transmit and handle various stimuli. In everyday life humans often use the *indirect pathway* to make important decisions. That is, emotional stimuli are routed through the core (especially via an area called the thalamus), to the shell/cortex (which analyses them). The cortex then sends appropriate responses to a core area called the amygdala. These pathways are illustrated in Figure 3.2.

This indirect pathway is slow, but it is precise, in that the data can be carefully scrutinized before being acted upon. Humans have this unique ability in that they can use the cortex to sort out various complicated emotions and perceptions and make good decisions in carrying out their responses (behaviors).

However, a lot of times this flow of emotional data gets "short circuited" through the *direct pathway*, entirely bypassing the cortex. Emotional stimuli automatically trigger responses with the cortex being totally left out. The result is a very fast response, based largely on emotions and without much thought or logic going on. While lightning fast, the downside of this direct pathway is that it offers only a very crude analysis of the incoming data.

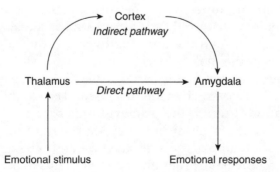

Figure 3.2 The two pathways for managing emotional stimuli.

For example, imagine you are a lost hiker trying to find your way out of the wilderness. You are out of water and are slowly becoming dehydrated under the blazing hot sun. As you continue on your way looking for rescue, out of the corner of your eye you see a large snake. Immediately you are frightened. You stop and prepare to flee. After all, the last thing you need right now is a bite from a poisonous snake.

But then, as you look closer, you realize that is no snake at all. It turns out to be a root that has somewhat the shape, size, and color of a snake! No longer frightened, you continue on your way—until you remember that roots have moisture in them. Moisture you desperately need. You run back over to the root, pick it up, and start chewing on it. What you first perceived as a danger turned out to be a godsend.

Your first reaction to the stimulus, to stop and prepare to flee, used the very crude, but very fast, direct pathway in the brain, the one where the cortex is left out. But eventually your cortex caught up: you employed the indirect pathway in your brain, and hence you were able process more detailed information and make a better judgment call.

Of course, if it *had* been a large poisonous snake, you would have been very grateful for the crude and fast direct pathway. So it really is nice to have a healthy balance of both of these systems working at all times.

That is, it takes both the logical brain and the emotional brain (along with healthy doses of wisdom, experience, and just plain luck) to be successful at finding your way out of a wilderness . . . and into successful market trading!

But there are times when the cortex gets left out, or at most does not get involved until after a decision has already been made and executed through the rapid pathway. In the case of the lost hiker, for example, he could very well have dashed away in the opposite direction before his cortex realized that it was a root and not a snake. In a case such as this, the fast and crude short-circuiting of information through the primeval region of the brain can be harmful. This improper or untimely short-circuiting through the direct pathway happens to even the best and wisest of brains. In fact, some people have programmed their brains to act in this manner on a regular basis.

The good news and most important message of this chapter is this: the shell part of your brain can be trained to better sense, interpret, and use raw emotions, as well as to modulate its own responses to them. This type of training is called cognitive behavioral therapy (CBT), and we will have an entire chapter discussing it, including the newest and hottest form of cognitive therapy, called CBM: cognitive bias modification.

Some people may need to learn how to temper or limit their emotional reactions, while others may need to learn how to tap into them better. That is, some individuals have probably trained their brains to depend too heavily on the indirect pathway, always looking for a logical answer.

Take for example *Star Trek's* Mr. Spock. Totally devoid of emotion and relying purely on logic, he would probably never have survived in the real world (let alone market trading). While calmly analyzing the percentage chances of being eaten by that saber-toothed tiger about to attack him, he'd already have been devoured for lunch!

Most of us are not like Mr. Spock. For most of us the ingrained power of the older and deeper parts of the brain (our emotions) often and easily overpowers the logical, analytical, and newer parts of the brain. And it is for this reason that traders find themselves doing things that make no logical sense in retrospect but that make perfect emotional sense at the time.

This pattern (emotions getting in the way of sound logical thinking) is just part of being human and how we developed as a species. The point is not to get rid of our emotions entirely but to appreciate and understand them, manage them better, and tap into them when that is called for. We don't want our feelings to dominate or control our God-given human intelligence and ability to think logically, but we equally don't want our emotions to be totally squashed or ignored by our intellect. Pure rationality with no appreciation of emotions can be just as deadly for your trading as sheer emotion, unbridled and unchecked by sound reasoning. Remember, when there really is a poisonous snake or tiger crossing your pathway, you do want your anxiety to take over you and cause you to jump back!

George Soros, regardless if you agree with his political beliefs or not, certainly has been one of the better hedge-fund managers and traders of modern times. In his 1995 book, *Soros on Soros: Staying Ahead of the Curve,* he describes how he would make trading decisions based on when he would get a backache.

> I rely a great deal on animal instincts. When I was actively running the fund, I suffered from backache. I used the onset of acute pain as a signal that there was something wrong in my portfolio. The backache didn't tell me what was wrong—you know, lower back for short positions, left shoulder for currencies—but it did prompt me to look for something amiss when I might not have done so otherwise.[1]

Soros is not nuts when he says this. What he may or may not have clearly understood is that his back is directly connected to his brain by nerves and that emotional stress or dysregulation in his brain can indeed cause somatic or bodily sensations, such as pain, GI symptoms, and so forth. In fact, there is a whole field of medicine devoted to the study of the two-way highway between the brain and the body: psychosomatic medicine.

Anyway, the point is that emotions (a.k.a. "gut feelings," sensations, and so on) are very important and should not be ignored altogether. Figuring out how to appreciate, decipher, manage, and use your raw emotions to your advantage is very, very important to successful trading.

Just how important are gut feelings? The nerve that connects your gut to your brain is called the vagus nerve, a.k.a. the tenth cranial nerve. It turns out that about 80–90 percent of the fibers in the vagus nerve are afferent (relaying data toward the brain) and only 10 percent are efferent (sending data away from the brain). More simply put, the vast majority of the traffic on the highway that runs between the gut (as well as other organs) and the brain is, in fact, going toward the brain, and only a small portion is travelling away from the brain. So, quite literally, your gut is feeding neuronal information to your brain all the time and in huge quantities. Your gut loves to talk to your brain. To an extent, it probably pays to listen to your gut when trading!

Of course too much of a good things is never good. Although they have a very legitimate role in every investor's arsenal, intuition and gut feelings perceived and mediated by the deeper aspects of your brain should always play a subordinate role to, and should never dominate, the CEO of your brain (that is, the cortex).

Canadian journalist and author Malcolm Gladwell has sold millions of copies of his book *Blink: The Power of Thinking Without Thinking* (2005)[2], in which he proposes that quick and spontaneous (impulsive) decisions can be just as good as carefully planned, deliberate and analytically derived decisions. While he is certainly a very popular pseudoscientist, Gladwell is by no means an academic or a researcher. His theories clearly start to break down and prove themselves flawed if applied to trading the markets or other forms of complex, high-stakes, fast-paced emotional-rollercoaster activities.

In a rebuttal to Gladwell's book, journalist Michael LeGault wrote *Think: Why Crucial Decisions Can't Be Made in the Blink of an Eye* (2006).[3] Unlike Gladwell, LeGault argues in *Think* that America (and indeed the entire Western culture) is in decline because of a current intellectual crisis. LeGault asserts that snap and spontaneous decisions are detrimental to our society; he maintains that relying on emotion and gut instinct, instead of critical reasoning and facts, is ultimately a threat to our freedom and way of life.

The truth, of course, is that humans have to adeptly use and combine both their intuitive and their analytical powers if they want to succeed at anything, including market investments. You, as a trader, need to draw on both anatomical areas of your brain: the shell and the core. You need to feel *and* you need to think. The challenge is to strike the right balance between thinking and feeling at any given moment.

The human brain . . . what a mighty machine. Although it only comprises about 2 percent of your total body weight, your brain actually consumes 20 percent of the oxygen you breathe in and 20 percent of the total calories you burn. There is a myth that you only use 10 percent of your brain. You actually use your whole brain all the time—it's just that you are not aware of most of your brain's activity and function. It's not like 90 percent of your brain is lying dormant and wasting away, waiting for you to find a magic switch to turn it on. That's a pipe dream: that somehow, if you could tap into and harness the dormant 90 percent of your brain, you would be 10 times as productive, smart, clever, or what have you.

What this 90 percent number really means is that the vast majority of what is going on around you at any given moment is filtered out and totally ignored by the 10 percent of your brain that is aware of things. Your body's mainframe cannot afford to waste time or energy on interpreting meaningless information and background noise. Your brain would go into information overload if it had to devote equal attention and energy to every single stimulus that it could possibly pick up from your various senses.

The deeper core of the brain does a lot of the unconscious filtering out, deciding what is important for your higher brain to make sense of and act upon. This deeper brain structure sounds an alarm any time it senses something out of the ordinary, and it alerts the cortex to it. By first filtering out the millions upon millions of stimuli that are going on and, for the most part, remaining the same around you, your core can bring to your shell's attention any changes or anything unexpected in front of you.

There is one more key anatomical area of the brain we need to map out in this chapter in order for the rest of the book to make sense. Buried deep in the brain's core is a structure called the nucleus accumbens. What is important to know about this structure is that it's the seat of reward, pleasure, and addictive behaviors. Both basic and more luxurious (motivated) rewards (such as food, drink, sex, shelter, pleasant aromas, music, pretty faces, drugs, and so on) create "feel-good" experiences by activating neurons in the nucleus accumbens. These neurons are programmed to deliver "shots" of the feel-good neurotransmitter dopamine every time they are activated.

The nucleus accumbens is essential for the survival of our species. Turn off pleasure, and you basically turn off the will to live. However, chronic or excessive stimulation of the brain's pleasure center drives the process of addictive behaviors, and with prolonged stimulation of these neurons, the signal attenuates and gets weaker. Consequently you have to consume/take/do more of the same "drug" to get the same effect—you are building up tolerance. And so you consume more.

You can probably see, then, how the nucleus accumbens figures prominently in the brain of an unregulated investor or a gambler who is enjoying these activities because of the pleasurable sensation they bring. And you can see how this vicious cycle, once activated, can be hard to break.

The key thing for traders to realize about the nucleus accumbens is that money (or, more specifically, the desire or idea of making money) causes the neurons in this reward network to fire like wild. Again, this deep-brain network was created and designed with a clear and useful purpose in mind: survival of the species. And although it runs on and is enhanced by pleasure derived from sex, good food, or being successful at doing something, its neurons can easily be hijacked by excessive behavior and lead to disaster.

Interestingly, research has shown that this reward network in the brain gets especially excited about the anticipation of rewards, even more so than the rewards themselves! It turns out that the thrill of anticipating rewards (looking forward to having good sex, a delicious meal, or making money) is actually more stimulating to the reward system and brings more euphoria than the actual achieving or fulfilling of those things. So our reward system actually rewards us for wanting to capture uncertain rewards and to take risks to do so. Ironically, this means it also causes us to expect that the future will be more wonderful than it actually is, once it arrives. Basically, our brains are tricking us into a reinforcing reward system that never quite meets our expectations.

Think of the heroin addict who, upon seeing an empty syringe at the doctor's office, begins to feel intense and irresistible cravings to use some dope. Just the mere sight of this visual cue causes the addict to feel a rush of euphoria in his nucleus accumbens and the rest of the reward pathway. The reward pathway in this addict has become a runaway train: The developed behavior of "shooting up" is throwing fuel onto the fire by continuing to reinforce the reward pathway. At some point the heroin addict may not even get much of a "high" any more from using the drug, but the reward system is so hyperactive that he still has a huge urge to use whenever he sees the syringe or has other cues presented to him (social cues, for instance).

As we will see later in this book, this reward network (which we all come prewired with) can become especially problematic for futures traders who are trading for the sole purpose of getting a rush out of trading. Their anticipation and reward circuits get carried away. These traders will start placing trades in response to their own set of cues, when, in fact, they should not be placing a trade at all. And it turns out (as we shall see) that some traders are more likely to take on this maladaptive behavior than others. Their personality profile puts them at greater risk of falling prey to the vicious cycle of throwing fuel onto the positive-feedback system of rewards, and this, in the end, diverts them from making money in the markets.

Naturally there is a lot more to the anatomy of the human brain than what you just read; again, this is a gross oversimplification. But these are the essential points you will need to know as you read the rest of this book and apply it to your market trading.

Mental Edge Tips
- Striking the right balance between logic and emotion is paramount.
- Don't let your raw and unexamined emotions get in the way of your logical, deductive, analytical thinking, and likewise don't let your innate Mr. Spock get in the way of your gut feelings and intuitions. There will be times for each!
- Your brain's reward center is designed to trick you into thinking that pleasures will be more enjoyable than the anticipation of them. This is an extremely strong reinforcing pathway and can become very problematic for some traders.

CHAPTER 4

The Four Perspectives of Mental Life

The most helpful model for understanding human mental symptoms and conditions was developed at the Johns Hopkins Hospital by Dr. Paul R. McHugh and Dr. Phillip R. Slavney. At its core, this model recognizes that there are four standard methods, or perspectives, for viewing any aspect of the human mind or mental life and where it goes awry.[1] Each of these perspectives, like a facet of a crystal, can illuminate various aspects of a person's mind, either individually or together as a whole. These four perspectives (disease perspective, dimensional perspective, behavioral perspective, and life-story perspective), each in its own right, can find utility with identifying and rectifying different mental-life conditions or situations.

To better learn about human personality traits (and in particular, those of great traders), I will now briefly delineate the four perspectives. This will give you the context you need to study personality.

THE DISEASE PERSPECTIVE

The disease perspective deals with actual mental illnesses (diseases) and impairments that have, at the root, an identifiable abnormality in some brain structure or that structure's function. That is, in a disease there is a "broken part" (or a "broken function") in the brain that can be pinpointed. We are likewise able to identify the pathophysiology associated with the broken part, meaning we understand how the broken part leads to the symptoms of the disease. As with all somatic (bodily) diseases, the hope is for mental diseases to be prevented or cured. Various diseases of the mind include: major depressive disorder, bipolar disorder, schizophrenia, the various forms of dementia, and so on.

THE LIFE STORY PERSPECTIVE

The life story perspective explains how mental-life phenomena can arise as a result of stressful life events that happen to an individual. Examples here include: a rape victim who can't sleep at night, a mother who is depressed (grieving) after having lost her newborn infant, or a combat soldier who develops flashbacks and hyperarousal symptoms after witnessing a violent and life-threatening trauma on the battlefield. In cases such as these there is nothing intrinsically wrong with the brain in question (there is no broken part). Rather, normal and healthy brains placed under excessively stressful *extrinsic* situations can produce changes in any of the three components of mental life we talked about in Chapter 1 (mood, thoughts, or behaviors).

THE BEHAVIORAL PERSPECTIVE

The behavioral perspective takes note that goal-directed and goal-driven features of human life can take on pathological features. Eating disorders, alcohol and drug abuse disorders, sexual disorders, and so on can best be viewed through this facet of the crystal. Through the behavioral perspective we can identify physiological drives, conditioned learning, and an individual's free choice to do something (or to not do it). We can see how a behavior is initiated, and we can go on to explain what factors are involved in reinforcing and intensifying it. The initiation and reinforcement of gambling disorders (and, yes, that also includes addictions related to trading the markets) can best be seen through this perspective.

THE DIMENSIONAL PERSPECTIVE

This is the perspective we will be using for most of the rest of this book. The dimensional perspective promotes the concept that certain aspects of human mental life occur with quantitative gradation. That is, they occur on a spectrum. Unlike a disease (which you either have or you don't) a dimensional trait is something that every living person has to one extent or another. It's not whether you have it or not, but *how much* of it you have in comparison to everyone else.

There are many physical traits we commonly think of in dimensional terms. A great example is how tall someone is. Everyone has a certain height; even the shortest man in the world has some height to him. If you had the patience to measure the height of a billion people from all over the globe, you could plot the results on a dimensional graph. Designating the X axis for height and the Y axis for number of people, the data will give you a classic bell-shaped curve, as shown in Figure 4.1.

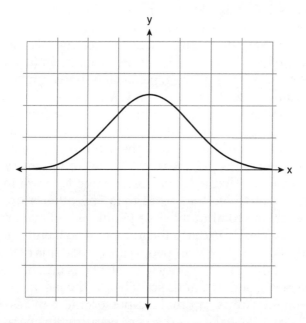

Figure 4.1 Dimensional features can be plotted along an X–Y axis and yield a nice bell-shaped cure. The greatest value indicated on the Y axis represents the median, and distribution drops off gradually the further away you get from the median in either direction.

The tallest people are on the right extreme of the curve, the shortest are on the left extreme, and the average height is right in the middle of the bell. With a *dimensional trait* (no matter if it is physical or psychological in nature) every human can be represented somewhere along the bell-shaped curve.

A *categorical trait* (think disease perspective) is different. It is something you either have or you don't; it's not on a spectrum. A clear example of a categorical physical trait would be a baby born with an extra finger on one of her hands.

Mental traits such as personality, maturity, and intelligence are dimensional and not categorical in nature. Just as with height, weight, or degree of skin pigmentation, we all have these traits to some degree or another. As such, mental traits can be measured using various scales or tests. As with height, when the results are plotted out on a graph they, too, will produce a uniform, bell-shaped curve. The peak of the bell is where the greatest number of people is to be found; this is the average, or the "mean." The number of people decreases smoothly and uniformly with distance away from the mean. Notice that there are no spikes or sudden dips anywhere along the curve. For example, human intelligence can be measured using a standardized IQ test, and a score of 100 is the mean (average) IQ of the entire population. Likewise, personality traits can be measured using instruments, and they too always yield a bell-shaped curve.

An important feature to highlight right up front is that it is not necessarily "good" or "bad" to be on one side of a dimensional scale. And although the mean is the score or measure with the greatest number of people, the reality is that almost everyone is not perfectly average. That is, 100 is the average IQ score in humans, and more people have that score than any other score for their IQ. However, the total number of people who have an IQ score other than 100 clearly exceeds the number who have an IQ score of exactly 100. Bottom line: Most people are on one side of the mean or the other. Another practical way to think of it is this: half of us score above the mean, and half of us score below the mean.

Personality traits can make a person more or less prone to mental distress, mistakes, and so on, because of several different factors. First and foremost is the *relative* position a person may have in any psychological dimension. The further away one is from the population's mean, the more vulnerable that person is to certain problems. Again, it's not only important which side of the average you come down on, right or left, but how far away you are from average score.

Take for example mental retardation (this term is less frequently used by professionals nowadays, but is well understood in the common vernacular; it is defined as someone having an IQ below 70). Obviously, mentally retarded people have a decreased capacity to solve problems, and this can result in very serious, real-life consequences. Clearly a person with mental retardation may not be able to figure out how to escape from an emergency situation (such as exiting a house that is on fire). The further to the left that person is on the bell-shaped curve (the lower the IQ), the more evident these problems become. This goes without saying.

But did you know that mentally retarded people actually have some *advantages* over people with normal or even high IQs? For instance, a mentally retarded person has a significantly lower suicide probability compared to someone with a higher level of intelligence. The reason is that mentally retarded people have less of a cognitive reserve to apply to contemplating life's problems; they just don't sit around thinking about the problems in their life. Plus, their low intelligence also makes it harder for them to plot sophisticated, lethal ways of "escape." So in this sense, their limited intellect is a protective factor against suicide.

The point is that dimensional traits can all be measured on a spectrum and that there is no such thing as being on the right or wrong side of the median, especially when it comes to personality traits. Substantially more critical is how far away you are from the median, how aware you are of your traits, how alert you are to the vulnerabilities your traits imply, and how experienced you are in adapting to your traits, so that you can maximize your strengths and minimize your weaknesses. So while there may be a "winning personality" in terms of successful market trading, this is not to say that everyone else has a losing personality and can never be expected to be profitable with trading endeavors!

Let's go back to the physical dimension of height. A very tall person, such as retired NBA player Yao Ming, may realize he has a certain dimensional attribute (height) in a certain quantity (very much) that might enable him to have advantages over others in a given situation. This extreme trait could be worth millions of dollars (as in playing basketball), or at the very least, this great height is going to be very helpful when it comes to reaching for a jar of strawberry jam off the top shelf of the supermarket.

But these giants better learn early to duck their heads when passing through doorways or they are surely going to lead lives filled with headaches. And imagine how agonizing it must be to try to buy clothes that fit right or to fly across the country in a coach seat if you are as tall as Yao Ming.

Incredibly short-statured people, on the other hand, have to learn to adapt to the benefits and drawbacks associated with their stature. Meanwhile, people who are of average height don't spend that much time thinking or worrying about or adapting to their height; height is not really an issue for them, one way or the other.

Mental Edge Tips
- Personality is all about dimensions. The simple example of extreme height variation in a basketball player is one we can use to understand dimensional attributes. We can all picture in our mind's eye a very tall NBA player making millions of dollars because he can slam dunk the ball and easily pull down rebounds. But he still has to stoop every time he walks through a doorway and he is not able to get the clothes he sees when he goes to the mall, regardless of how much loot he has in his pocket. Exactly the same principles apply to personality traits.
- Successfully adapting to your own personality traits is all about identifying the extremes, acknowledging them and how they get in the way, and then learning to positively adapt to them. As you read through this book, keep referring back to these basic concepts.

CHAPTER 5

Introduction to Personality Traits

Personality traits can be defined as dimensions of individual differences in tendencies to show consistent patterns of thoughts, feelings, and actions. Just as people differ along a spectrum in terms of their cognitive capacities (IQ), age, weight, and height, so too do all people vary in their proneness to certain ideas, moods, and drives.

For instance, some people are innately more emotionally stable and calm, while others are more emotionally labile. Some people are more trusting (perhaps even to the extreme of being naive and prone to being exploited by others), while others are not trusting at all (and hence have few close interactions with others). A person can be optimistic versus pessimistic, dependent versus independent, detail-oriented versus carefree, and so on.

In everyday language all of us frequently describe the temperaments of the people we know and interact with using various adjectives. "He's an agreeable guy," or, "She is so gregarious." In fact, a review of the Oxford English Dictionary finds that there are well over 4,400 different adjectives that can be used to describe human personality traits. Although each of these adjectives is an attempt to describe a personality trait, not every adjective is a personality trait in itself. There are three criteria that must be met for something to be a true personality trait:

1. Enduring—it must not change significantly with time.
2. Pervasive—it must show a consistent pattern across many situations and aspects of life.
3. Distinctive—it must be easily described, assessed, and understood.

Sometimes a particular personality trait is so evident in a person that even the most untrained eye can see it. At other times these traits are inherent, but much more latent, attributes that only can be identified under specific circumstances, that is, when a latent personality trait is brought into play by some challenge or provocation.

Again, as with height or intelligence, all the various human temperamental traits plot out neatly in a smooth and graded fashion around a mean average (that is, the traits of a large number of individuals yield a bell-shaped curve).

The summation of one's personality traits leads to what can best be described as a personality "type." Even the ancient Greeks noted four major personality dispositions: sanguine, choleric, melancholic, and phlegmatic. The Greeks thought that four different bodily fluids affect human personality traits and behaviors. Sanguine (blood) referred to the pleasure-seeking and sociable personality, the choleric (yellow bile) individual was ambitious and leaderlike, melancholic (black bile) people were seen as introverted and thoughtful, while those with a relaxed and quiet temperament were labeled by the Greeks as phlegmatic (phlegm). The great Greek physician Hippocrates (460–370 BC) incorporated the four basic human temperaments into his medical theories. From the time of Hippocrates until now, these four temperaments, or slight modifications of them, have been part and parcel of many theories of medicine, psychology, and literature.

People who have personality traits that cluster in a certain type to such an extreme that it frequently results in interpersonal difficulties are said to have a personality "disorder" of one form or another. For example, histrionic personality disorder (previously known as hysterical personality disorder) is defined by extreme emotional lability, self-centeredness, attention-seeking behaviors, flamboyancy, sexual inappropriateness, and shallow self-dramatization.

Besides just grouping and naming personality types, it is important to realize that we can also identify a person's tendencies to react to circumstances in a particular emotional fashion. Of course we cannot predict with 100 percent certainty how someone with a particular temperament will respond to a specific provocation, but we are able to see that groups of people with certain personality traits tend to think, act, and feel in similar patterns. This is critical to understand.

Consider this analogy using human intelligence: It is impossible to precisely predict which specific questions a high-school student with a particular IQ will miss on her SAT exam. However, we can predict that the students with the highest IQs, in general, will outperform all the other students. We also can predict that the smartest kids will, in general, fare better on the tougher problems. We can even make a fairly educated and accurate prediction of a particular student's overall score based on her known IQ.

But of course there are many other variables besides raw intelligence that will come into play on exam day, such as what she had for breakfast, how well she slept the night before, how much she studied and retained, and how motivated she is to do well on her exam. Taking into account all these other variables, we can predict with a good deal of reliability which students will perform the best on their SAT. But it takes just one of these other factors to throw our best predictions off. If the student test-taker comes down sick on exam day, for instance, all bets that she will perform at her expected level, given her known IQ, are off.

Likewise, we can predict with some degree of certainty how people with certain personality traits and vulnerabilities will respond or react, given a certain challenge or stressful situation, but there are also plenty of other variables that make bullet-proof predictions impossible.

This brings up another very important point. In general, a person's unique set of personality traits is generally stable across time. The propensity is for personality to endure and not change much as one ages. Once a person's brain is fully developed and no longer physically growing (on average this occurs at about age 23), his or her personality traits are—for the most part—determined. They are not exactly set in stone, but they are very hard to change. (We will come back to this critical point in a later chapter, with some evidence that points to the fact that personality *can* be modified a bit; but for now, be aware of this: since we have little means to change our temperament, our only remaining choice is to better understand it, experience how it affects our lives, and then try our best to adapt to it for the better.)

Given that there are well over 4,000 different words in the English language that can be used to describe a person's personality, this could lead one to wonder, are they all equally important? Is there some way to discern which personality monikers are most scientifically useful in describing people and in predicting how they will act, feel, or think in certain situations?

Hans Eysenck (1916–1997) was a German-British psychologist and the first "big name" in personality testing. He is still considered the grandfather of modern personality analysis. He applied the statistical process known as *factor analysis* to human personalities to tease out which traits are most relevant and verifiable. Factor analysis is just a fancy word for using mathematics and statistics to see which things (in this case adjectives describing people) tend to clump together. For example, the adjectives "gregarious," "talkative," and "sociable" are not very different from each other. We would expect that those people who are gregarious are also talkative and sociable.

In one of his key early experiments, done in 1947, Eysenck studied the personality traits of enlisted military men. Using a factorial study of the intercorrelations of various traits, he discovered that the two major dimensions of personality variation are:

1. Neuroticism (N)
2. Extraversion (E)

N and E are often referred to as "the big two." Interestingly, these were the same personality dimensions that had already been described, at least theoretically, by earlier psychologists, such as Carl Jung. Indeed, research dating back to the 1930s by MacDougall and Thurstone had already demonstrated "five factors" of personality—a topic to which we will return in greater detail. But

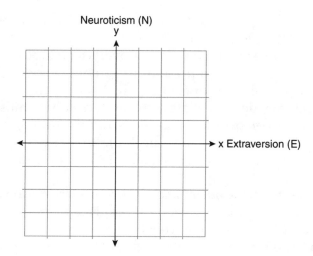

Figure 5.1 Plotting two different personality traits on an X-Y axis: neuroticism and extraversion.

it was Eysenck who was first able to statistically show (based on data, not just theory) that there are two main human personality traits (N and E). For this his name has gone down in history as the foremost pioneer in modern personality research.

It can be very helpful to plot personality on an X–Y axis. Let's do that with neuroticism (N) and extraversion (E), as shown in Figure 5.1.

In brief, the trait of extraversion (denoted here by the X axis) refers to the *speed* at which someone experiences his emotional reactions, and in particular, positive emotions. Recollecting the bell-shaped curve we discussed earlier, we can divide the entire population into two groups: those who are on the right of the mean (extroverts) and those who are to the left of the mean (introverts).

What does it mean to be high in extraversion (E)? It does not simply mean someone who is the life of the party. It really refers to someone whose positive emotions, in response to triggers or various life stressors, come on very rapidly and likewise dissipate very rapidly. (Hence, these people are the life of the party because they quickly warm up to others around them.)

Extroverts also relate to the present implications of events. Thus, they often do not plan ahead or prepare for consequences. Basically they live in the moment. Extroverts tend to be more social, warm, and responsive to present life circumstances. Extroverts have an "external locus of control," which basically means they look for external devices to make themselves happy (music, dancing, sports, other people, or perhaps more pathological external devices, such as drugs and alcohol). When things go wrong, extroverts tend to place external blame instead of taking personal responsibility.

Introverts, on the other hand, are low in extraversion (E). They tend to have slow, or even delayed, positive emotional responses to life events. They are more cool and slow to warm up in social situations. Their emotions come on gradually and also tend to leave that way. They have an "internal locus of control": They tend to look more inside of themselves for the source of their happiness and meaning (prayer, meditation, contemplation). Also, introverts relate better to the future or past implications of events. They find it difficult to be living in the moment and can have trouble appreciating what is happening right now because of their propensity to overly focus on what happened in the past or what may happen in the future.

Extroverts are more influenced by rewards (that is, they respond well to positive feedback), while introverts are more influenced by punishments (they respond well to constructive criticism) and hence are more prompt in developing conditioned reflexes.

The neuroticism (N) dimension (denoted in Figure 5.1 by the Y axis), on the other hand, deals with the *strength and depth* of emotional reactions a person has to life stressors or triggers. It especially relates to negative emotions, including anger, anxiety, guilt, and depression. Emotionally, a more neurotic person responds intensely to life events, while the less neurotic responds weakly. To be sure, the words "neurotic," "neurosis," and "neuroticism" can be problematic. For one thing, the meaning of these terms has changed somewhat over the last century. Also, in the common vernacular the word *neurotic* often refers to more of a continual internal angst or anxiety, or a conflict-driven person. When hearing the word neurotic, people may summon up an image of Woody Allen, perpetually fidgety and flustered. But that is not quite what psychologists and psychiatrists currently mean when they use this word and its derivatives.

For instance, a highly neurotic person could be an emotionally stable person at baseline and under normal circumstances, but then dramatically come unglued under pressure. The neurotic, in the context of some life stressors, experiences strong emotional reactions (especially negative ones).

Let me paint a picture of an extreme neurotic. Imagine that an individual is driving along to work, feeling no particular emotions at all, when he comes to a stoplight and is suddenly rear-ended at low speed by a total stranger. In response to this episode of minor inconvenience, his emotions "explode" like a bomb with anger. He goes "ballistic" like a missile. He exits his vehicle screaming and yelling, hurling expletives, and fuming. In fact, so violently has his anger erupted that he's not even able to perform the basic tasks that we all have been taught to do in this kind of fender-bender situation (pull to the side of the road, exchange insurance information, look for a witness, take a picture, and so on). His exaggerated emotional response is now impairing his ability to function properly and logically do the right thing. Immediately prior to the accident, this neurotic would have been totally logical and had good mental capacity, but now his emotions have totally overridden things. Until he calms down, this neurotic is going to make some mistakes and needs to be careful.

Take the same scenario, but imagine instead this time our driver is very low in neuroticism. Instead of flying off the handle, the driver gets out of his car cool, calm, and collected. He proceeds to do all the right things, very respectfully exchanging insurance information with the other driver and then goes on his way without even showing a sign of emotionality. His negative emotions are clearly more stable under stress.

For this reason we sometimes prefer to use the words "stable" and "unstable" when discussing the neuroticism personality dimension, although this designation might also imply that one side of the mean is "good" and the other side is "bad."

The truth is (just as in the example of the seven-foot basketball player in Chapter 4) that there can actually be advantages to being a little "neurotic" in temperament. Likewise, being a little too "stable" can land you in hot water if you are not careful. So if, after you take a standardized personality test, you find out that you are on the "unstable and neurotic" side of this particular bell-shaped curve, remind yourself that, since half the human population is there too, it can't be all bad.

Here's another important concept to register as you learn about personality. Traits such as extraversion and neuroticism are orthogonal. This means that your position on one of these personality dimensions has no bearing on and does not predict your position on any of the other dimensions. It also means that for any two dimensions being compared, they will divide a population of people into four separate groups, or subcategories (represented by each of the four quadrants on the graph shown in Figure 5.2). Hence, a person may fall into the "unstable (neurotic) extrovert" group, while someone else may be in the "stable introvert" group or one of the other groups represented by the other two quadrants. If fact, it turns out that the four quadrants delineated by these "big two" personality dimensions (neuroticism and extraversion) equate to the four main personality types first described by the ancient Greeks!

We come back soon to these "big two" dimensions (extraversion and neuroticism) in much more detail in subsequent chapters.

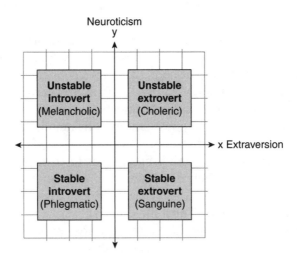

Figure 5.2 Four main personality groups are delineated by orthogonally plotting neuroticism versus extraversion on an X-Y axis.

Mental Edge Tips
- Be aware that statistical analysis shows that certain human personality traits are much more important and evident on a mathematical basis than others and that these traits apply to the entire population of human beings. We can plot them out on a bell-shaped curve, and for any one person we can measure how far away he or she is from the average (mean) score.
- Neuroticism and extraversion are the "big two" personality traits. And by plotting these traits on an X–Y axis, we obtain four personality types (one for each quadrant).
- Neuroticism refers to the strength of one's emotional responses under stress, especially negative ones. Extraversion refers to the speed of one's emotional responses, especially positive ones.
- There is no "right side" of the mean. Remind yourself again that the critical thing is how far away you are from the mean, and how you are dealing with it.

CHAPTER 6

Where Does Personality Come From?

There has existed a debate among psychologists for some time about where somebody gets his or her personality. One camp argues for the "trait theory," which states that internal factors (think genetics) are what shape a person's temperamental makeup. The opposing side of the argument holds to the "social learning theory," that personality is molded by forces outside of the person, such as operant conditioning.

This is the classic question of "nature versus nurture," and it's a debate that can be held over pretty much any human condition (whether it's cancer, diabetes, or the common headache). Both what we are made up of (internal, genetics, and so on) and the environment (the external, what happens to us, what happens all around us, and so on) can potentially be involved in any human illnesses or conditions, and this also applies to personality.

The strongest evidence today points to both internal and external factors being vitally important in the creation of a person's personality. We cannot say that one carries more weight than the other. Studies have consistently shown that genetics account for about 45 to 50 percent of variation in human personality, while the balance is accounted for by forces and events that occur after one is born, and especially during the crucial developmental and formative stages of life, lasting from early childhood to early adolescence.

For example, research studies have shown that even neonates, newborns straight out of their mothers' wombs, have clear differences in autonomic reactivity and behavior when exposed to stress. There is also research demonstrating a strong hereditary component to personality in monozygotic twins (two people who came from one egg, hence sharing the same DNA) who are raised apart in different environments. But there is also a strong body of evidence demonstrating that healthy nurturing and guidance through experience instill a person's character, as well.

The reality is that, in every person, both internal and external forces contribute to the development of personality and should be assessed for their relative contributions to an individual's personality (and, more important, that person's vulnerability to distress and ability to manage situations that challenge him or her).

There are more and more clues coming out about personality and how it is formed. Functional magnetic resonance imaging (fMRI) allows neuroscientists to see exactly which regions and realms of the brain react to external stimuli and in some cases to what degree. Exciting research is going on that is allowing us to trace traits back to which part of the brain they are emanating from. This kind of scientific work helps us determine how humans interpret a given situation as being good or bad, risky or safe.

A research project out of Stanford University published in the journal *Science* shows that people will respond to a potentially pleasant object or experience in very different ways based on differences in personality.[1] The study looked at people with varying degrees of extraversion (E), as determined by formal personality testing. All of the participants in this study were shown multiple pictures of happy, sad, and angry faces while being scanned by an fMRI machine. All of the participants, both the extroverts and introverts, had a little pea-sized area of their deep brain (core), called the amygdala, light up whenever they saw a hostile or angry face. But only in the extroverts did the amygdala light up when sad faces were shown. This study may not seem like much, but it helps us understand that who we are as people (that is, our personalities) is clearly hard-wired into certain areas of our brain and is at least partly determined by biological causes. The brains of extroverts and introverts do not work in quite the same way.

And yet there is also plenty of research from the school of social psychology showing that personalities are shaped by societal and social situations that people find themselves in, and that they are affected and developed by personal histories. Or, as Shakespeare put it, "all the world's a stage, and all the men and women merely players." Meaning that we are what we play. We all take on and play many roles in society, and these social roles do, to some extent, shape our identity.

Each role we play brings with it certain rules or expectations about how we should behave and react in certain situations. A good research study demonstrating this was the famous "prison guards" experiment that looked at how people behave when arbitrarily assigned to roles as either a guard or a prisoner.

Mental Edge Tips
- Your personality, your identity, is shaped by both your genetics and your external life circumstances, especially those that occur while your brain is still developing (up until the early 20s).
- Again, we need to stress the point that you cannot alter the personality that you already have by very much. So you are going to have to learn to deal with it!

CHAPTER 7

Personality Inventories

A personality inventory is a test (usually a written, self-reported questionnaire) that attempts to reliably assess or measure various dimensional traits in people. They are intended to apply through-out the entire human population. These tests are structured, mean-ing they make use of direct questions about a person's opinions of himself. A good inventory always has unambiguous instructions about how to complete the test.

One very obvious weakness, and potential flaw, of all such self-reported personality tests is that the person completing the test, if she so chooses, can purposefully answer the questions incorrectly in an attempt to manipulate the results. The test administrator has no way of knowing for sure that the test-taker is not cheating or lying on the test, and hence the results are entirely dependent upon a sincere and truthful participant.

That's very different from a blood test, such as measuring the serum level of cardiac enzymes as is done to evaluate the likeli-hood of a heart attack. It would be quite hard to falsify the amount of cardiac enzymes that are floating around in one's bloodstream. However, this kind of intrinsic weakness is not entirely limited to psychological tests. Clearly there are many blood or urine tests that people often attempt to falsify (such as the professional athlete who is trying to avoid the detection of anabolic steroids).

Well-designed personality tests have built-in scales designed
to detect erroneous responses and to adjust scores accordingly. Even
then, any honest psychologist or psychiatrist will freely admit that
a personality test is only as accurate as the person who is "bubbling
in" the answers.

Using personality tests is becoming more and more com-
monplace, even outside of the clinical arena. A recent study by
the American Management Association found that 39 percent of
all companies surveyed use personality testing as part of their hir-
ing process. These personality inventories are also frequently used
in evaluating potential business partners, finding spouses, room-
mates, and so on. Attorneys occasionally use these tests to analyze
criminal behavior, witness examination, and jury selection.

Personality testing is not all fun and games, though. In one
noteworthy court case, (*Wilson v. Johnson & Johnson*) the jury
awarded the plaintiff $4.7 million dollars after it was found that the
plaintiff's former employer had caused psychological harm by having him take repeated, and even excessive, personality tests. Wilson
claimed that the repeated scrutiny of his personality caused emotional strain, personal grief, and even a nervous breakdown.

Another risk or danger of personality testing is that a participant who is not psychologically strong may come to rely on the
results in negative ways. The subject may make assumptions about
how he should react in certain situations. That is, he could possibly
become complacent about his own personality traits and become
overly dependent on the textbook descriptions associated with
his personality type. Someone who is not aware of the limits and
inherent self-simplification that personality tests can foster could
potentially be harmed by such testing.

There are dozens of different personality inventories created
by different people, but all are designed to objectively measure
personality in adults. And while it is true that multiple theoretical and technical differences exist between the different personality
inventories, there is converging evidence that they are measuring
the same basic traits (albeit sometimes named differently).

Just to reiterate, the most important traits assessed by any
personality test are those in which the test-taker deviates to an
extreme. No two humans are alike, and it is most essential to look
for "outlier scores" when it comes time to assess which traits are
most important, or problematic, for a person. Therefore, the most

useful inventories are the ones that give quantitative assessments of personality. Typological tests, which are those that classify people into various personality types but do not give any kind of measure or degree, are less helpful.

Another important point about personality testing is that, no matter how long and detailed a test may be, it can never assess a certain trait in all circumstances. That is, personality, and the associated reactions one has to life events, may not always be consistent across all situations. At times it can be situation-specific.

To give an example, a person may score very high in the trait of impulsivity, but she may not be an impulsive person in all of life's contexts, just most. She might be more impulsive when it comes to deciding what to eat (that piece of chocolate cake she can't resist), but less impulsive about spontaneously buying a new piece of clothing every time she turns on the television shopping network. In general an impulsive person is going to demonstrate impulsivity in multiple domains of life, but not always!

Another very consequential aspect of personality tests is that they are *not* valid on individuals who have altered or deranged mental states caused by a mental illness, intoxication, or whatnot. These tests should only be taken by the mentally healthy and fit. If you are presently suffering from a mental illness and are either untreated or undertreated, you should not take a personality test. The results will reflect more of your illness and not who you are in your premorbid (healthy) state. If you are (or even think you are) presently suffering from major depression, mania, anxiety, or psychosis, do the right thing. Seek the help of a professional. Once you are well and back to your normal self, you can have your personality tested. For now, get treatment for your illness.

Here are a few of the more commonly used personality inventories, as well as some of their strengths and weaknesses.

MYERS-BRIGGS TYPE INDICATOR (MBTI)

The Myers-Briggs Type Indicator is widely used on online dating sites and for other forums of pop psychology. It is based on Carl Jung's psychological types and was developed during World War II by Isabel Myers and Katherine Briggs. However, at least half of the published research behind this instrument was not done independently (it was carried out solely by the company that markets it), and hence it has a reputation for being less critically validated. Another huge negative is that it is a typological test: It only tells you what type of personality you have (of sixteen different types) and does not tell you how mild or how extreme your traits are in comparison to the general population.

MINNESOTA MULTIPHASIC PERSONALITY INVENTORY (MMPI)

The Minnesota Multiphasic Personality Inventory (and its revision the MMPI-2) provides a wide range of data on numerous personality variables and is backed by a strong research base. However, it tends to emphasize major psychopathology (people with personality disorders) and is not as useful for individuals with more moderate or mild personality tendencies. The MMPI and MMPI-2 can also provide discrepant results. These tests are also considered biased toward the upper socioeconomic status and are not validated in adolescents.

EYESENCK PERSONALITY INVENTORY (EPI)

The Eyesenck Personality Inventory uses a true/false format, is useful as a screening tool, and is backed by a theoretical basis. The test questions are transparent as to purpose. It is generally not recommended for anything other than a screening device.

REVISED NEO PERSONALITY INVENTORY (NEO PI-R™)

The Revised NEO Personality Inventory, also known as the NEO-AC, is the most researched, reliable, and validated personality test available today. It is also the one to be described and referred back to in the rest of this manual.

Mental Edge Tip
- It is impossible for personality tests to be as specific as we would like them to be. They are imperfect tools, but tools nonetheless. For this reason, personality tests (and other psychological tools) are really only intended to be administered, graded, and interpreted by skilled professionals who are aware of their limitations and even their possible dangers.

CHAPTER 8

Introduction to the NEO PI-R

The Revised NEO Personality Inventory, NEO PI-R, is the gold standard of personality testing. It will be referred to here (as it is in many other places) simply as the NEO-AC.

The NEO-AC was developed by two psychologists, Drs. Costa and McCrae, in 1985, and then revised in 1992. It is composed of 240 self-report questions that are answered on a five-point scale (from strongly agree to strongly disagree). Each question is written so that anyone with a sixth-grade reading level will be able to take the exam. On average the test takes approximately 40 minutes to complete (though there is no time limit in taking it). Questions of test-takers can be answered by the person administering the test, if necessary, to clarify definitions, meanings, and so on. Although some of the questions on the test may sound similar to one another, there are actually no "overlapping items," and the scales are balanced to control for acquiescence.

The questions on the NEO-AC are, in and of themselves, not very "deep" and don't carry much weight outside of their use in assessing your traits compared to other people who read and answer the same set of questions. That is, after you have taken the test and find out where your personality traits line up in comparison to others who took the test, there is no point in going back to the questions and trying to interpret why you answered one question one way or another question another way.

One of our traders who took the test commented, "The questions were somewhat contradictory. One question asked me if I like bright colors and flashy items. I like bright colors, but don't like flashy items, so how do you answer it?" Again, the exact content of the question is not so important as how you react and respond to that question in comparison with everyone else who has ever taken the test. Don't get stressed out if you think a question is poorly written or you aren't sure what the question is really trying to probe. The questions may seem arbitrary or contradictory, but actually each one is very carefully crafted and precisely worded in a way so that, in large numbers, the test always produces a "bell-shaped curve" for each of the traits. So when taking the NEO-AC, try not to overthink or psychoanalyze things. Simply read the questions, take them at face value, and answer them, one after another, as honestly as you can.

The name NEO-AC comes from the fact that this test is assessing the five major personality domains. These are also sometimes termed the "five factors" or the "five- factor model" (FFM):

N—Neuroticism
E—Extraversion
O—Openness
A—Agreeableness
C—Conscientiousness

Each of these five major factors is composed of six separate facets, or subfactors. Hence, in total the NEO-AC assesses thirty distinct personality traits. Taken together, the NEO-AC's five domain scales and thirty facet scales facilitate a comprehensive and detailed assessment of normal adult personality. Both paper and computer forms of the test are available. The test must be administered by a trained professional, and the test and its contents are all copyrighted material.

There is also a short version of the test, called the NEO-FFI, which only has 60 questions and takes less than 15 minutes to complete. However, this short version only looks at the five major domains and does not get into the facet level.

One commonly heard criticism of the NEO-AC is that it's a test of limited scope and does not explain all of human personality.

Some psychologists argue that the test overlooks personality traits, such as motivation, thriftiness, sense of humor, and so forth. However, the very reason that not all personality traits are included in this test is that these other traits were either (1) not validated as occurring in a bell-shaped pattern across all cultures and peoples, (2) not stable enough, or (3) not easily described or measured in a simple pen-and-paper test.

Although the NEO-AC is not perfect, it is the best tool out there for assessing personality. It is concise, accurate, and well validated. And that is why it is the test routinely being used by researchers and scientists trying to learn about personality and how the mind works. It is the test used in massive amounts of data published in high-level academic journals. The NEO-AC is truly recognized around the world as the gold standard for personality assessment.

Other important attributes of the NEO-AC include:

- It is usable in both clinical populations (diagnosis and treatment of personality disorders) and the general population (employment screening, for instance). Pathological personalities are related to normal variations in basic personality, making this tool applicable to everyone.
- It uses the "Five Factor Model" (FFM), which is the product of two independent and convergent streams of research dating back to the 1930s (adjective ratings and inventories/questionnaires.) It builds upon the work of MacDougall, Thurstone, Cattell, Eysenck, and others.
- It is based in strong psychological theory but is presented in lay vocabulary.
- It is the most validated personality assessment, backed by the most robust research. It has been shown to have temporal stability and consensual (cross-observer) validation.
- It has been related to all the other major models in the psychological literature.
- It has proven universality (it can be applied across age, sex, and culture).

- It has a biological basis and has been backed by heritability/genetic studies, as well as neurobiological and pharmacotherapy studies.

The NEO-AC is backed by multiple research studies demonstrating:

- Internal consistency. Coefficient alfas for the individual facet scales ranged from 0.56 to 0.81 in self reports and from 0.60 to 0.90 in observer ratings.
- Retest reliability. Using a sample size of N = 2,274, both 6- and 9-year stability coefficients were demonstrated for all 5 of the main personality factors.
- Factorial invariance.
- Convergent and discriminate validity, including correlations with other personality tests and correlations with adjective lists.
- Consensual validation.
- Construct validity: The NEO-AC has the ability to predict multiple relevant criteria in people. These include: overall psychological well being, coping and defense methods, needs and motivations, Jungian types of personality, interpersonal traits, openness, creativity, divergent thinking, temperament, and hypnotizability.

Some additional tips follow.

Mental Edge Tips
- To get full value out of the rest of this book, you will have to have your own personality assessed using the NEO-AC. It truly is the only personality test you should be taking.
- When taking the NEO-AC, just answer the question to the best of your ability. If you have already read this book or studied a lot about the 30 facets, try to avoid thinking about how you are answering the test questions or which facet is being probed. Just answer the questions with as much sincerity and honesty as you can. The risk here is that your answers may be a little biased if you have insight into what the test questions are probing.

- When taking the NEO-AC, your "top of mind thoughts" are what we are trying to measure, not your subconscious mind. You should never have to spend more than a few seconds on the questions. Don't try to make yourself look good on your answers, because that will only falsify the results and work against your interests to discover who you really are.
- The NEO-AC is hands-down the most validated, reliable, and research-proven personality inventory in existence today. It is the tool that clinical psychologists and researchers turn to most when they need to accurately and easily assess a person's temperament.

CHAPTER 9

The Five-Factor Model in Detail

The NEO-AC takes its name from the five-factor model (FFM) of personality. Again, we can easily see where the NEO-AC gets its name:

1. Neuroticism (N)
2. Extroversion (E)
3. Openness (O)
4. Agreeableness (A)
5. Conscientiousness (C)

In your mind's eye right now you should be summoning up the image of the bell-shaped curve. Each one of these five major factors can be plotted as just such a curve. Also, you should bring back to mind the image of the X-Y axis. Just as we were able to plot out N versus E, so too can we plot any two of these five main factors of personality against one another, with the intersection of the two axes representing the median of two bell-shaped curves.

For example, if you were to measure everyone in the world for both openness (O) and agreeableness (A) and plotted the data out on an X-Y graph, you would develop two bell-shaped curves, one for each axis. Around the X-Y intersection is where the most number of people would be found, and fewer and fewer people would be located further out along the X and Y axes. See Figure 9.1

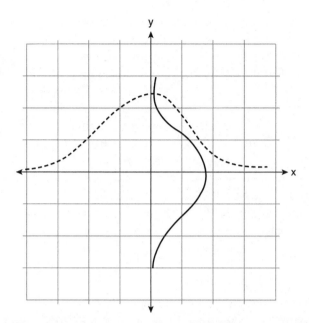

Figure 9.1 Overlapping bell-shaped curves. This figure shows how two personality traits can be plotted one against the other. The result is four distinct quadrants. Can you see how very few people will be at the extremes of both traits? That is, most people can be found around the intersection of the X and Y axes, and very few are found far from both the X and Y axes.

For any one of these five domains you can be considered and measured as either being "average," "high," "very high," "low," or "very low." Again, how far away you are from the mean is what determines if you are high or low in any one personality trait.

Here are brief descriptions of the five major personality domains, broken down by severity of score (notice how very high and very low scores are problematic and can become even "pathological"):

Neuroticism
- People *high in N* have a tendency to experience strong and deep emotions—especially negative ones such as anxiety, anger, guilt, shame, sadness, embarrassment, and disgust.

- Those *very high in N* are prone to chronic negative feelings (anxiety, depression, fearfulness, tension, irritability, anger, dejection, shame, guilt, hopelessness) and overall emotional instability. They can develop irrational beliefs. For example, they can have unrealistic expectations or they can place perfectionistic demands on themselves. They cope with stress more poorly than other people. They can have unfounded somatic complaints, such as chronic pain or other physical symptoms that have no identifiable physical causes. They can feel helpless and tend to seek out others for emotional support and decision making, and as such, can become dependent or needy. They have difficulty inhibiting impulses (such as eating, drinking, smoking, taking drugs or spending money). They have trouble accepting criticism. They tend to form unstable relationships.
- People *low in the N* dimension are emotionally stable. They are able to remain calm under pressure and are generally even-tempered and relaxed. They are able to face stressful situations without becoming rattled or upset.
- Those *very low in N* can lack appropriate concern for potential problems (in social, health, and other realms), due to their emotional blandness. They tend to have too much emotional control, and as such, miss out on life and tend to repel others. To their own detriment, they don't pick up on their own emotional cues.

Extraversion
- Individuals *high in E*, extroverts, warm up quickly and are sociable. They prefer large groups and gatherings, are assertive, active, and talkative. They generally do not function well if left alone and to their own devices. They like excitement and seek external stimulation and external sources of happiness. They tend to be cheerful and warm in disposition. They live in the moment, ignoring the past and not planning on the future. People high in E also have a tendency for rapid onset of emotions. Their emotions also quickly dissipate. They have difficulty spending time alone.

- People *very high in E* can be prone to excessive talking, leading to inappropriate self-disclosure and social friction. They have great difficulty spending time alone. They are prone to reckless excitement-seeking, attention-seeking, and overly dramatic expressions of emotions. This can lead to inappropriate attempts to dominate others. They can be sexually promiscuous.
- Those who are *low in E,* introverts, are reserved (though they are not unfriendly and still have friends). Their emotions come on slowly and likewise leave slowly, compared to those of others. They are independent, rather than being either leaders or followers, and can have a reluctance to assert themselves. They are even-paced rather than sluggish, and they have a preference to be alone and like internal stimulation and internal sources of happiness. They reflect on the past and plan for the future.
- Those *very low in E* can have social isolation and interpersonal detachment, and lack joy or a zest for life. They can be prone to depression. They may be reluctant to assert themselves or assume a leadership role, even when they are fully qualified. They often do not have active or satisfying sexual lives.

Openness
- People who are *high in O* have active imaginations, are intellectually curious, and are open to new experiences. They can be eccentric at times. They prefer variety as opposed to the mundane or routine. They are willing to entertain novel ideas and unconventional values. They have a good deal of aesthetic or artistic sensitivity. They are attentive (attuned) to their feelings, being able to appreciate both positive and negative emotions more keenly.
- Those *very high in O* lack practicality and often have unshakable eccentric beliefs (ghosts, UFOs, reincarnation, mystical powers), can be prone to accepting false ideas or being taken advantage of or duped by others. They can become overly preoccupied with fantasy and

daydreaming. They can have a diffuse self-identify (may join a cult) and frequently change goals in life. They can be susceptible to nightmares and altered states of consciousness. Their rebelliousness and nonconformity can interfere with social or vocational advancement. They often feel like outsiders.

- Those who are *low in O* are rigid, conventional, and conservative in outlook. They prefer the familiar to the novel.

- Those *very low in O* can have great difficulty in adapting to social and personal change, and they have a low tolerance for different points of view or lifestyles. They can have a muted appreciation and poor understanding of their own emotional responses and feelings, and they also have trouble verbalizing their feelings to others. They have a constricted range of interests, have an insensitivity to art and beauty, and show excessive conformity to authority. They have stereotypical beliefs and expectations. They are uncreative and unimaginative.

Agreeableness
- People *high in A* have good interpersonal tendencies. They are trusting of others and are altruistic. They like cooperation and are sympathetic to the plights of others. They are eager to help others and believe that others will be equally helpful in return.

- Those *very high in A* can be gullible and can indiscriminately trust others or follow the lead of others. They can be excessively candid or generous to the detriment of self-interest. They can have an inability to stand up to others and fight back, and as such, are easily taken advantage of.

- People *low in A* are egocentric. They are skeptical and suspicious of others' intentions. They are competitive, not cooperative. They can be antagonistic and tough-minded.

- Those *very low in A* can be exploitive and manipulative. They can endorse cynicism and paranoid thinking. They can have difficulty trusting even their own family and friends. They can be quarrelsome and too ready to pick fights. They often turn to lying. They can be rude and inconsiderate to the point of alienating their own friends and limiting their social support system. They have a lack of respect for social conventions, which can lead to troubles with the law. They tend to have an inflated and grandiose sense of self, and they are arrogant.

Conscientiousness
- Those with *high* C scores are noted for their orderliness and punctuality. They have superior organizing and planning skills. They like to carry out tasks to their completion. These people are purposeful, strong-willed, and determined in life. They are also industrious. Multiple research studies have shown that high C is strongly associated with and predictive of both academic and occupational achievement.
- Those with *very high in* C may be annoyingly fastidious and compulsive. These are the overachievers and the workaholics who are overly-absorbed in their jobs (or some other causes they have), to the exclusion of family, social, and other personal interests. They can be overscrupulous in moral behavior and excessively clean and tidy. They are bound to pay too much attention to detail, to the point that they miss the big picture (they can't see the forest for the trees). They have a pattern of being overly rigid, and they have difficulty seeing that there are times when it is to their own benefit to set work tasks aside in order to relax and have fun.
- Individuals *low in* C, conversely, are very casual people. They are poor planners. Others will see them as being disorganized and unreliable. They can also show poor self-control.
- Those *very low in* C have poor academic performance and are underachievers, leading to personal and occupational aimlessness. They do not fulfill their intellectual or artistic potential. They also tend to disregard rules, conventions, and responsibilities, and this can lead to trouble with the law. They are unable to discipline themselves (stick to a diet or exercise plan, keep promises, and so forth). Those most

low in C can even be unable to discipline themselves when medically required, and hence their problematic habits lead to medical problems that could have been avoided.

As you read the above descriptions of the five main dimensions, or factors, of personality, it should become readily apparent to you that there is not necessarily a "right" or "wrong" side to any of these temperamental traits. Rather, it is the degree away from the average (mean) that is critical, and how that trait plays out in certain situations.

For example, someone who is very high in openness (O) may be prone to being sold a false bill of goods. You can expect that, on average, those poor and unsuspecting souls who fell victim to the gigantic Ponzi scheme of Bernie Madoff were quite high in the openness domain. Although greed for a high return on their investments was probably also a major contributing factor, by and large Madoff's investors were not dumb people who didn't know any better. Most of them probably were aware the promised return was unrealistic, and probably a good number of them had already heard about previous Ponzi schemes from watching episodes of *60 Minutes*. More likely they were just "too open" to an investment idea that many other people would have turned down as being "too good to be true," and it got them in trouble. But surely these same people who are high in O have also had this particular trait work to their advantage at times in their life, as well. Maybe because of this trait, they have gotten in on the ground floor of some investments that turned out to be real winners and not scams!

Mental Edge Tips
- It's not which side of the spectrum (dimension) your personality lies on. Rather, it's how far away you are from the average that matters, and more important, what you make of it! The farther away you are from the mean, the more problematic any given trait is going to be.
- The wise learn to take full advantage or their personality traits. They know the limitations and vulnerabilities of their personalities and are able to make positive adaptations to their behaviors, expectations, and emotional responses.

CHAPTER 10

The 30 Personality Facets

Each of the five dimensional domains (factors) in the NEO-AC is composed of six separate subfactors, or traits. These traits are referred to as the "facets" of personality. Like the five major domains, the facets are also dimensional in quality (for each one you can draw a bell-shaped curve showing a smooth and even distribution around a mean).

Appendix A provides detailed descriptions of the 30 facets, but here is a brief list of these facets of personality to review before proceeding further:

Neuroticism
- N1: Anxiety
- N2: Angry hostility
- N3: Depression
- N4: Self-consciousness
- N5: Impulsivity
- N6: Vulnerability

Extraversion
- E1: Warmth
- E2: Gregariousness
- E3: Assertiveness
- E4: Activity

- E5: Excitement-seeking
- E6: Positive emotions

Openness
- O1: Fantasy
- O2: Aesthetics
- O3: Feelings
- O4: Actions
- O5: Ideas
- O6: Values

Agreeableness
- A1: Trust
- A2: Straightforwardness
- A3: Altruism
- A4: Compliance
- A5: Modesty
- A6: Tender-mindedness

Conscientiousness
- C1: Competence
- C2: Order
- C3: Dutifulness
- C4: Achievement striving
- C5: Self-discipline
- C6: Deliberation

These 30 facets, although they do not represent every single possible personality characteristic (such a test would be too long and cumbersome—again, there are over 4,000 adjectives listed in the dictionary), are the most consequential traits and the ones that can be consistently verified by research and also cross-verified using various other personality tools.

Using the description of personality according to the six personality facets that comprise each major domain, a trained psychologist or psychiatrist can look at these results and tell you many interesting things about who you are, what you like, what careers would fit you well, and yes, even the type of person you should seek in a romantic relationship. It is also using these 30 facets that we will explore the minds of great futures traders.

CHAPTER 11

General Interpretation
of NEO-AC Scores

When interpreting the results of a person's completed NEO-AC test, it is important to remember that this tool is based on a top-down, or hierarchical, assessment. The first step is to look at the pervasive trends in the more broad domains (the five major factors), and to find out in which of these five factors the person most deviates from the mean. The second step is to analyze each subdomain (facet) to identify those that are contributing most to the overall major domain score.

What this means is that the five major domains always "pull rank," compared to the individual facets. For example, if it turns out that a person scores "low" on one of the five major domains (let's say on the Openness factor), but happens to score "very high" on one of the subdomains (let's say on facet O3: Feelings), the more relevant result is always going to be the one for the major domain. This is *not* to say that the isolated "very high" score on O3 is unimportant or has no useful applications. Indeed, it is very important. But, in general, always consider domains first, and then look at facets.

A person's NEO-AC numerical scores, both in the five major domains and in the thirty facets that make up the domains, are usually tabulated and plotted on an "Adult Norms Profile Sheet."

The Norms Sheet is copyrighted material and therefore is not repro-
duced in this book. However, if you have taken the NEO-AC, your
results will be plotted on a Norms Sheet for you, and this is what you
will be using and referring back to as you read the rest of this book.

The norms are valid for all adults aged 21 and up. A separate Norms Sheet is available for those test takers between ages
17 and 21. The NEO-AC has not been validated and should not be
used in individuals younger than 17, at which time personality is
still being molded and shaped. Also, as has been known since the
start of time that men and women differ in their personality traits,
and hence a different set of norms applies to each gender.

The adult Norms Sheet is basically a numerical representation
of the bell-shaped curve we discussed earlier. For those of you who
are statistically minded, the norms have been constructed to allow
for conversion from raw scores to *T scores*. T scores have a mean
of 50 and a full standard deviation of 10. Therefore, 68.26 percent
of all test takers will fall within the first standard deviation from
the mean (T scores between 40 and 60); 95.44 percent of test takers
will fall within two standards deviation from the mean (T scores
between 30 and 70); and 99.72 percent of all test takers will fall
within three standards of deviation from the mean (T scores
between 20 and 80).

For the layperson, it is easier to think in terms of severity, not
T scores. The Adult Norms Profile Sheet, to this end, categorizes
all domain and facet scores as falling into one of five descriptive
categories:

> Very High
> High
> Average
> Low
> Very Low

The first step in interpreting NEO-AC scores is to identify all
of the outlier scores, that is, those scores in the very high or very low
zones. These are the traits that, by and large, can be most problematic and need the most attention. Scores in the average range can
generally be ignored, whereas those in the high or low range are
moderately important.

CHAPTER 12

Personality Styles

Just as before, when we plotted neuroticism (N) versus extraversion (E) on X–Y axes, plotting any two of the five main dimensions of personality one against the other in such a manner will yield four different quadrants. The sum total of the four quadrants is referred to as a *personality style*. Which of the four quadrants a person falls into will determine the nature of his or her personality style.

For example, let's plot Conscientious (C) on the X axis and Openness (O) on the Y axis. For shorthand, we can denote high scores with a positive (+) sign and low scores with a minus (–) sign. Doing so, we get the result shown in Figure 12.1.

By plotting out the five main factors against one another, we arrive at a total of ten different personality styles:

Style of Well Being (N and E)
Style of Defense (N and O)
Style of Interests (E and O)
Style of Anger Control (N and A)
Style of Impulse Control (N and C)
Style of Interactions (E and A)
Style of Activity (E and C)
Style of Attitudes (O and A)
Style of Learning (O and C)
Style of Character (A and C)

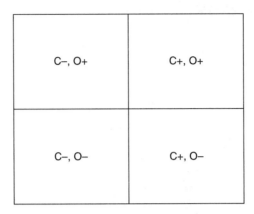

Figure 12.1 Plotting C against O yields four quadrants of a personality style.

Although any two main domains can be plotted, special interest is paid to plotting the most pronounced traits (those traits that deviate most from the mean). For example, if a person is found to be very high in one domain (let's say A) and very low in another domain (let's say C) but is average in all the other domains, then clearly these are the two domains we want to plot out on the X–Y axes in order to look at a personality style. It can still be fun and maybe even useful, to look at and meld those scores that are in the "high-average" or "low-average" range, but really we want to start with the outlier domains when interpreting personality styles.

For a full description of the 10 personality styles, please see Appendix B.

CHAPTER 13

Personality Disorders

The term *personality disorder* is a term used clinically by psychiatrists and psychologists to indicate that a person has maladaptive variants of personality traits. People with personality disorders continue to repeat maladaptive behaviors, thoughts, feelings, attitudes, defenses, and so on, even though this obviously results in social and occupational consequences. The personality disorders, by affecting interpersonal relationship so severely, can be extremely disruptive in a person's life and cause enormous amounts of suffering. Individuals with personality disorders are unable to manage their traits on their own and require intensive psychotherapy and sometimes even medications. People without personality disorders, in contrast, are able to learn from negative experiences and change their behaviors, thoughts, and feelings in order to avoid negative consequences in the future.

The maladaptive symptoms, patterns, and traits of the personality disorders are listed and described in detail in the psychiatric taxonomy book, *The Diagnostic and Statistics Manual*, fourth edition (DSM-IV), and will not be repeated here. There are a total of 10 DSM-IV personality disorders. What is important to understand is that the five dimensions in the NEO-AC are empirically related to personality disorders and their symptoms. It is also important to realize that personality disorders are merely extremely maladaptive and extreme variants of normal personality traits that everyone has.

TABLE 13.1

Five of the Personality Disorders and Their Facet Scores

Personality Disorder	High Facet Scores	Low Facet Scores
Narcissistic	N2, N4, O1, C3	A3, A5, A6
Borderline	N1, N2, N3, N4, N5, N6	A1, A4, C1
Avoidant	N1, N3, N4, N6	E2, E3, E5
Obsessive-Compulsive	E3, C1, C2, C3, C4	E6, O6, A4
Antisocial	N2, E5	A2, A3, A4, A6, C3, C5, C6

Each personality disorder yields a unique set of extreme scores on various NEO-AC facets. Table 13.1 shows a few examples of how facet scores cluster in personality disorders.

CHAPTER 14

Neuroticism and Trading

If you have stayed with me through the first 13 chapters, you should now have a basic understanding of personality traits. But you did not buy this book just to learn about personality. The real question you want answered is: Which personality traits make for successful trading? And the follow-up question you likely have is: What can I do to adapt my personality to be more like the personality of successful traders?

We already know that it is unfeasible—if not downright impossible—to significantly change your personality. But even so, wouldn't you still like to know if there is a certain personality profile that successful market traders have? Are there certain traits that make for better trading? Because if there are, maybe it is possible for you to adapt or modulate yourself to compensate or take into account your weaknesses and take full advantage of your strengths.

Again, this is a key principal: We cannot significantly change who we are, but based on our life experiences (good and bad) and our deepening appreciation of ourselves, we are able to learn to adapt in a healthy and beneficial way. Learning about what makes for a great trader is the first step, as it gives us something to compare ourselves to.

We will first turn our attention to neuroticism and trading. Neuroticism is one of the "big two" domains, as you know from the previous chapters. But when it comes to traders, it should probably be called "the big one." That is, this domain comes into play the most frequently, for better or for worse, in the lives of active traders.

A 2005 research study by Lo, Repin, and Steenbarger[1] looked at the personality traits and emotions in a group of 80 volunteers—all high-frequency futures day traders who had enrolled in a trading seminar. Some of these traders were novices, while others were more experienced. So it was a real mixed bag of traders. For one entire month, the study participants filled out daily mood surveys that rated their emotional states as well as their ongoing trading performance. The results showed a clear connection between the degree of emotional reactivity, as measured on the daily surveys, and how successful a trader was during that month, as measured by normalized profits and losses. The daily mood ratings clearly showed that those traders who had more controlled emotional reactions to the markets fared better in the profit and loss column. Meanwhile, those traders who experienced more intense and reactive emotions displayed significantly worse trading success. Of note, this result applied to *both* positive and negative emotions; that is, overall significantly poorer trading performance was seen in those traders who experienced either positive emotions (happiness, joy, pleasure) after winning trades or negative emotions (anger, anxiety, depression, vulnerability) after losing trades.

The authors of the study were quite perplexed, however, because they also obtained NEO-AC personality testing on all 80 of the research subjects, and it turned out that they found *no* correlation between successful trading and an individual's level of neuroticism. Nor was there a connection between any of the other four main personality domains and trading success.

So what's going on here? Why was their no correlation between trading success and neuroticism? Well, for one thing, it should be mentioned that, in this study, they used the simplified version of the NEO-AC, which does not break down the five main factors into the 30 individual facets (again, there are six facets to each of the five main factors). So is it possible that, by using the more detailed NEO-AC that breaks neuroticism down into its components, that something could be garnered that the simple NEO fails to show?

Or is it that Lo's study had too few participants ("not powered up in size") to really show any patterns?

A 2011 MarketPsych LLC report issued by Richard Peterson and coauthors also looked at personality testing in investors.[2] In his unpublished white paper, Peterson reported on 2,600 investors who took an online version of the simplified NEO-AC test. It is not clear what kinds of investors are included in this study (long term versus short term, stocks, mutual funds, futures, or what), and it is assumed that a hodgepodge of people likely completed this free, quick, and easily accessed online test. Peterson admits in his report that there is no way to verify whether the people who took his test accurately and honestly reported their financial success as investors. Nevertheless, the results from this very large study showed that low neuroticism (as well as high openness) had the highest correlation to successful investing. While contradicting Lo's earlier findings, the sheer size of this study does tend to lend it more credibility.

Why is it that "cool cucumbers" (people low in N) in Peterson's study appear to be making more money? The reasoning harkens back the diagram in Chapter 3 depicting the direct and indirect circuits of the brain. Even-tempered, emotionally stable, and mellow traders are able to continue to carry on making logically sound decisions, after either winning or losing trades. Neither the excitement from a recent slam dunk trade nor the shame, sadness, anxiety, and anger of a recent defeat are blinding these people's better cognitive judgment on the next set of decisions they need to make. Simply put, they are better equipped at handling the emotional rollercoaster ups and downs that cause others to panic or make other rash decisions based on emotions alone. Equally important, they likely don't let those emotions originating outside the trading world (marital strife, for instance) get in their way of trading. Their cognitive prowess and critical thinking skills are not being short-circuited or overrun by their emotions.

So the research already out in the public domain lends itself to the idea that one's emotional state while trading is vitally important. Any strong or reactive emotional response is counterproductive. Emotionally reacting to either winning or losing trades is likely going to have a negative impact on your success in the markets. And that makes common sense.

Why? Because trading the markets is not a form of gambling, so much as it is a form of art and an intellectual pursuit. In pure gambling, luck (chance) is the predominant force in deciding who wins and who loses. Trading the markets, on the other hand, makes frequent use of those higher, cognitive brain functions (such as logical reasoning, mathematical computations, recognition of patterns and trends on a graph or in a table, short- and long-term planning, executive decision making, and so on). Your ability to use these higher brain functions (which are carried out in the cortical regions of your frontal lobes) can easily be "short-circuited" by strong emotional reactions that are taking place in much deeper areas of your brain (the limbic lobe). Those traders who are able to limit the influence of the limbic lobe on their frontal lobe, according to the research, are more successful in trading the markets.

The 2005 and 2011 studies mentioned above certainly caught our interest, but we wanted to delve deeper into this matter. My father and I decided to do a study of our own. We decided to give the *full-length* version of the NEO-AC personality inventory, but only to a group of top-notch, extremely successful futures traders from around the world. We wanted to learn if there are certain personality traits that the world's best traders share, and, if so, how we can apply that body of knowledge to better understand ourselves and achieve more prosperity in our own trading.

Unlike the research project above that looked at a group of traders of differing or even unknown levels of experience and investing results, we specifically and carefully hand-selected a cohort (group) of traders that has consistently demonstrated an ability to succeed at trading the futures markets for years, if not decades. These are traders who have managed large sums of money, won trading championships, and so on. Real traders with real track records of success. Initially we started this research out of curiosity, with my dad being the first to take the test. But eventually, as we discussed with traders their results, they encouraged us to further share the results, and the idea of this book was born.

So, do you want to know the results of our research? Of course you do. We found that the total neuroticism score (N) for our cohort of very successful traders was actually average, just as was found in the 2005 study by Lo! Are you surprised? Did you anticipate it was going to be low? We did.

That's right; at first blush it appears these great traders are not quite the cool cucumbers we had expected they would be. They don't appear to be raging neurotics with emotions that erupt like Vesuvius, but they are also not the most emotionally stable group either.

But when we look at neuroticism on the facet level, we find some very interesting results, indeed. It turns out that these winning traders routinely fared quite a bit lower on two of the N facets: N1 (anxiety) and N6 (vulnerability). That is, these successful traders, compared to the average people walking around on the street, experience far less anxiety and feel far less vulnerable to failure and defeat when they are placed under stress. There were no such clear patterns with the other N facets. In fact, in order to make an overall average N score in this population, some of the other N facets were a bit higher than average!

So, it would make sense that learning how to manage and control feelings of anxiety and vulnerability under stress may potentially lead any trader (including you)—no matter where he rated on the N1 and N6 facets—to better profits in the markets. But how to do that? If you are someone who scored higher up the ladder in either of those two facets, N1 and N6, pay special attention!

Moving beyond the raw data scores from the NEO-AC test, we also engaged some of our research subjects in some in-depth psychological interviewing. From our discussions with these stellar traders, it became clear to us that it is not just how emotionally reactive someone is under stress, but more, important, how well she is able to regulate and manage that reactivity when it comes up that is critical.

Although in our study most of the top traders have low N1 and N6 scores, not all of them did. And it was the several stellar traders who did *not* have low N1 or N6 scores that fascinated me most, and these are the ones when I interviewed in more depth, to find out how they are able to consistently be successful in the markets, despite being prone to anxiety and vulnerability.

The consensus was pretty consistent and clear. More emotionally reactive traders (that is, those with higher N1 and N6 scores) can—*with experience*—learn how to modulate the way their emotions ebb and flow in response to the markets. These are traders who have learned how to thrive *despite* being emotionally reactive creatures.

But enough of generalities; let's put some of this knowledge garnered by our top traders into practice and also see how it really applies to us.

Neuroticism, again, is the tendency to experience negative emotions, especially under stressful circumstances. Those traders who score higher in N are more prone to having their emotions interfere with their trading. Winning trades that bring excitement and pleasure may result in overconfidence, which can lead to reckless decision making on the next trade. Losing trades can instill fear, anger, and self-doubt, which can result in hesitation and possibly missing out on a prime move in the markets. Top traders consistently report that the anxiety they experience with trading has to do with (1) the fear over losing money, and (2) the fear of feeling embarrassed by being wrong.

A very successful trader took the NEO-AC, and his total N score was, interestingly enough, high at 97. Again, almost all of them had average N scores, so this guy was an exception to this rule. Most prominent in his case was an N2 anger-hostility score of 25 (nearly off the charts). With a score such as this, one would expect a tendency to become angry or hostile, either at those around him, or inwardly at himself depending on whether he was an introvert or extravert, of course. In this case he was an introvert.

An introverted person with this high an N2 score is prone to beat himself up over a losing trade, belittle himself, and over time, develop a low sense of self-esteem. He is vulnerable to taking out his anger on himself, or on the markets. He may fall into "revenge trading," whereby he is trying to regain money lost in a previous trade. This is like the tennis player who, having just lost a point after a very protracted and energy-depleting rally, now tries to overcompensate on her very next serve. Instead of serving as she has trained herself to do countless times (just the right amount of velocity, spin, and angle), she instead takes her anger out on the next serve. And of course she smashes the ball straight into the net with an incredible force, and she just lost another point, compounding the frustration. Those prone to anger need to find healthy ways to "vent" after a losing trade, before the initiation of the next trade.

Another trader, well known for his trading exploits, has a high depression (N3) score that has affected his trading at times. His story is interesting and educational enough that he agreed to have a whole chapter of this book devoted to his situation. Both of these "neurotic" traders have been very successful in the markets for long periods of time, despite some rather worrisome trait scores. But despite one or two personality traits seemingly stacked against them, they have (in one way or another) learned to recognize their weakness in neuroticism and adapted to it. They succeed despite these traits, not because of them.

The N1 (anxiety) facet deserves special attention when it comes to trading the markets. Again, our winning traders in general were low in N1. The primary anxiety of market trading revolves around the fear of losing money as well as the fear of being a failure. Nobody likes to lose money, granted. But in this high-stakes, fast-paced, and often (but not always!) unpredictable and tumultuous game we call market trading, those who rate high in N1 need to pay particular attention to their level of anxiety as they trade. The fear of losing money is huge and should never be trivialized; it is often what triggers a bad decision or diverts one's full attention from the logical process of assessing the markets. How many times have you gotten out of a small winning trade right before it turns into a big winner, all because you were fearful the market was going to turn against you?

Anxiety frequently involves the scrutiny of something that actually does not or should not need much thought at all. Think of the talented football wide receiver who "chokes" in the fourth quarter of the Super Bowl on a pass he normally could easily catch, even with his eyes closed. A routine and automatic act he has done thousands of times since childhood is suddenly upset and over-turned by being too aware of what he is doing in the moment. It only takes a nanosecond of distraction by fear for the preci-sion and timing of a complex football play to be totally blown to smithereens.

The kind of fear I am referring to right now is that of being judged by others. It is a fear of not being capable or not being up to the task of performing under pressure, when the chips are down and it really counts. Subtract the importance of the game, the noisy stadium crowd, and the fact that the whole world is watching on

TV, and the wide receiver would easily make the catch. But instead, he is too aware of the moment and the potential for fear, and he freezes up.

Of course when you are trading in the friendly confines of your own home, there is no national TV audience watching your every move in the markets. So this is not quite "performance anxiety" in the true sense of the disorder. Yet in another sense it is very much related to performance anxiety. Because every move you make while you trade is surely being watched by the harshest and most critical judge of all: yourself. In trading, generally you are the only one who is putting the immense pressure on yourself to succeed. Being your own judge, you can get yourself into some serious "mind games." As the saying goes, you turn into your own worst enemy.

A typical mistake that anxious traders make is exiting a winning trade too early. They have identified a very specific exit target (price), but for some reason they start doubting themselves and their ability to forecast what the market is doing. And then they abort their trade too early, over fear that if they don't take the small profit now, they may lose it all and more momentarily. What could have (and should have) been a big winner all of a sudden is cut down into a minor profit. And minor profits are not going to cover the big losses every trader (even the best ones) is bound to have from time to time.

How to solve this problem? Ask Jerry Rice: the greatest wide receiver of all time. I encourage you to read the speech that Jerry gave when he was inducted into the NFL Hall of Fame. It's very motivating. Here is the most important snippet from that speech:

> I'm here to tell you that the fear of failure is the engine that has driven me throughout my entire life. It flies in the faces of all these sports psychologists who say you have to let go of your fears to be successful and that negative thoughts will diminish performance. But not wanting to disappoint my parents, and later my coaches, teammates and fans, is what pushed me to be successful.

The fearless Jerry Rice admits that fear is what drove him! The only way to overcome the anxiety associated with performance is to keep performing the act or behavior over and over until, it is no longer anxiety-provoking. For Jerry Rice, it meant playing in lots of crucial games. You can be sure Jerry was far more comfortable with each subsequent big game, big stage, and big spotlight he was put in. You often will hear superstar athletes describe the experience of not hearing the noise of the audience or even feeling like things are moving in slow motion, when the pressure is really on. They are so focused on what they are doing that the fear and the things that should be causing fear are totally displaced from their minds.

The psychological term is "habituation." It means that the more you expose yourself to an anxiety (instead of trying to avoid it), the sooner your body will learn to deal with the anxiety, and the sooner the anxiety will dissipate. Once the anxiety has dissipated enough, it no longer severely affects your trading performance.

However, don't start with the Super Bowl. One of the main tenets of treating anxiety is to start with low anxiety-provoking situations and then continue to confront increasingly more stressful scenarios. Start with paper trading, of course. Then, as you start real trading, start with less volatile and scary markets. Start with small positions. Gradually and incrementally increase your risk as you get accustomed to each new level of trading anxiety. Use mental rehearsals and guided imagery to confront anxiety-provoking scenarios before tackling them in real time. That is, close your mind and imagine you are in a very stressful and anxiety-provoking trade. See yourself come through it intact and unscathed. The more you do this, the more your brain will habituate, and the easier it will be to teach your brain to develop healthy coping strategies to overcome anxiety. Soon it will become automatic.

Do you remember the first time you got behind the wheel of a car and tried to drive? Remember how anxious were you then? You were checking your rear view mirror every five seconds—to the detriment of not looking out the window in front of you! You dared not drive on the freeway, as that seemed way too fast and frightening. But over time, months or maybe years, you got so used to driving on the freeway that it became automatic. Today the biggest risk and fear in your driving habits is that of becoming so lackadaisical while driving on the freeway that you may miss your exit or fail to notice the idiot driver who is trying to change lanes next to you. Driving no longer seems scary—unless you are asked to sit in a car with a Formula One racecar driver, speeding around the track at speeds in excess of 200 MPH with other cars all around you doing the same thing, just inches away. Now that's scary, right? To you, yes. To the professional racecar driver, however, it's not. His mind has already become habituated to the fears of moving at 200 m.p.h.

Anxiety, it turns out, is all relative. It's nothing more than being confronted with a new scenario and not knowing how you are going to perform under these new sets of conditions. The only way to conquer it is to confront it and habituate to it.

The very worst thing you can do to treat your anxiety is to remove yourself from it, because you are denying your brain the chance to habituate. If every time you are in a winning trade you abort it early because you are starting to feel anxious and doubt yourself, you will never learn to trust your abilities (and intuitions). So you gotta stick it out, for better or worse. Don't abandon ship at the first heart palpitation or the first drop of sweat.

It can be a very uncomfortable process to force yourself to remain in an anxiety-provoking situation when your mind is telling you to get out of it. But it is the only way to overcome this problem. If every time Jerry Rice felt nervous in a big game he chose to sit out and just observe the action from the sidelines, he would never have learned how to become a big-game receiver. He would never have developed the ability to perform under pressure and master his emotions.

Therefore, do not flee anxiety.

Anxious traders tend to make other mistakes, too. If you ranked high in N1 (or any of the other N facets, for that matter), be sure not to set goals that are overly ambitious. You are only setting yourself up for disappointment and eventual failure. Your anxiety level will only *increase* if you do not meet your lofty goals, and that is the last thing you need.

Instead, try to avoid setting goals with dollar signs attached to them ("I aim to make $5,000 this month"), because if this month just happens to be an unlucky month and you don't reach your specified dollar goal, it may cause heightened negative emotions. That, in turn, will very likely spill over into poor trading performance during the next month, which perhaps could have been a good month . . . if only you had not become so emotional after missing your goals from the previous month. The result is now you have two bad months in a row! Our successful traders told us again and again that they are not focused on dollars when they trade.

Instead, create goals that are challenging and exciting, and yet still very attainable. Instead of promising yourself to make a set amount of money, set "process goals" ("I will make X number of entries this month," "I will monitor my trades with Y frequency during the day," "I will follow this trading system in Z market for the entire month"). Reassure yourself that, if you stop thinking in terms of only profit and loss and instead keep to these very concrete process goals, the profits are bound to eventually follow. This is what the successful traders report time and time again.

A very dangerous (and unfortunately all too real and too frequent) mistake that rookie anxious traders make is to overtrade. This is a huge source of losses. In fact, it's a bottomless pit of losses—a real Bermuda Triangle! Traders who are acutely and actively worried about their current financial situation (such as fears over not having enough to pay this month's mortgage, not making enough money to justify forgoing "a real job," or not having enough to pay for their kid's college tuition) can easily fall into the trap of trying to hit a homerun under less than favorable conditions.

At the risk of overusing the sports analogies, I'll ask you to think of playing baseball in a storm. It's rainy, it's cold, the wind is swirling around in all different directions, and the field is wet. This is no time to be swinging for the fences. Either take a rain check, or play a game that makes sense for the conditions. Hit singles. Look for defenders to make errors catching and throwing the ball. Play your strengths.

If you are fiscally behind the eight-ball, do not start increasing your hedges. Either get out of the markets and close your trading account, or come up with a strategy that will work under the current conditions. The all-too-commonly seen mistakes traders make when feeling fiscally anxious include getting into more contracts than they should (in order to solve their problems and reverse their losses all at once), trading when market volatility is low (grabbing for straws when what they really need is a life raft), trading when a pattern or indicator is only half there (launching a "Hail Mary," in the hope that something might miraculously come of it), trying to make up a losing trade with a quick rebound trade (like a "rebound relationship," this is just not going to work out well), and deviating from one's predetermined plan and strategy (don't start changing a known and reliable recipe for success).

As risk increases, so too does anxiety and the likelihood that you are going to make a stupid mistake. Take a basketball player shooting free throws. At the start of a game there is far less pressure, and it is easier to make a free throw. It just happens. But at the end of the game when the score is close and there are only a few seconds left in regulation, exactly the same shot becomes much more difficult—but only more difficult psychologically. It's still the same distance to the hoop, and the hoop is still the same diameter. But the research shows that the chances of missing a late-game free throw are much higher than they are for an early-game free throw.

Trying to manage 20 contracts, likewise, is very different, psychologically, from managing just one. One is far easier, because the stress is much lower. As more money and more of your self-esteem are at stake, the more you are going to feel nervous. With twenty contracts in play, you are far more likely to overanalyze the market or let your emotions distract you, even if for just an instant, culminating in a foolish mistake that you normally would not have made. The way to solve this problem is to titrate risk.

Titrate means to increase a dose (as of a medicine) slowly. Doctors often start medications slowly and then gradually ramp up the dose as the body gets accustomed to it and there are no side effects. Do the same thing in trading. Don't jump from trading single contracts one month to a dozen contracts the next month just because you are on a hot streak. Your anxiety level, no matter where your score is on N1, will not be able to tolerate it! Pace yourself, and build up emotional endurance in the markets.

But don't take all of this anxiety stuff too far, either. If you are feeling anxious about your trading and it is affecting your results (perhaps to the point where you wonder whether you will ever succeed again), don't jump to the conclusion that you have some deep-seated, hidden, or even subconscious psychological disturbance that needs to be uncovered before you can move on and succeed. Please, do not look up a hypnotist or psychoanalyst in the yellow pages! Likewise, don't rush to assume that all this anxiety you feel means that you need to "trash" your current trading style or systems and start with something totally new and fresh. Those are likely not the solutions to your problem, and if anything are only going to compound things. The real solution to your anxiety lies *in habituation* and *titration*, as described above.

For those high on the N1 anxiety scale, it will probably serve you well to avoid frequent checking of your trades, as this will probably only heighten your anxiety. But if you don't check up on you trades often enough, this too will be a source of worry. It is best to develop and then set predefined time intervals that result in minimal anxiety, and then train yourself to check only your active trades at those specified intervals (of course, always be sure you are trading with stops!). Strategizing and making a schedule like this makes you master of your anxiety!

A great way to do this is to start a journal wherein you rate the level of your anxiety at the end of each trading day. Separately, keep a log of every time you check your computer monitor, iPad, or any other device that gives you an update on your market positions. You are bound to see a pattern where peak anxiety occurs if you are either very rarely checking your trades or are checking them too frequently. Identify the middle ground, where anxiety is the least, and then stick to checking stocks only at the designated intervals. This will reduce negative emotional reactivity and make you a better trader.

Fear of losing money and of not performing up to your own expectations may be the most prominent anxieties traders routinely face, but they are certainly not the only ones. Another main one is fear of being proven either wrong or a deficient trader. Many traders have difficulty admitting to their spouses or others if they are in a bad trade. They may either deny it or minimize it. Not just because of the financial setback, but because it may reflect poorly on them as a person.

People who rate high on the N4 and N6 facets (self-consciousness and vulnerability) are particularly at risk for this kind of fear. It's an image thing—they are afraid to be shown up as poor or deficient traders. This can be a cruel form of psychological torture for those very high in N4 or N6 and can be especially damaging when the trader is so fearful about losing face that she starts denying to herself the extent of her losses. Usually unknowingly, she will fail to recognize obvious mistakes she is making in her trading behavior, because it is too distressful for her to come to the realization that she is wrong about something. It is often only after it is too late (her trading account has run dry) that she is able to step back and admit she was wrong about something in her trading strategy. So if you are high in N4 or N6, watch out for the perils of self-denial!

Being high in N5, impulsivity, probably speaks for itself. These are the people who are too trigger happy when it comes to entering (or exiting) a position. They give in to temptation. They don't do their due diligence. Or they may try to do their due diligence, but they still just can't wait, and they act prematurely. They think they might miss out on a good thing, so they impulsively make a snap decision before really investigating things. In the aftermath they realize, "Gosh, I forgot to think about variables X, Y, and Z." But take heart. One good thing about being high in impulsivity is that a good solution is usually readily evident (though not necessarily easy to follow).

Overtrading is one way to spot highly impulsive traders. Neglecting or even totally forgetting about active trades that they already have on, they take on more and more trades in an impulsive way. In real-life, individual trading (when you are your own boss and are responsible for all of your actions), each and every trade has to be cultivated, observed, managed, and eventually exited with great care. The greater the number of trades going on at once, the harder this is to do, and the more likely it is that you will make a costly mistake somewhere along the line. The impulsive trader gets in over his head in sheer number of trades simply because the temptation for one more "sure thing" trade is something he can't pass up. Often times overtrading occurs in volatile market conditions, when the impulsive trader feels he has to "do something" simply because the market is bouncing around and not because a particular buy or sell pattern is forming.

But the more you trade, the higher your costs. And the more you trade, the higher the likelihood that you will be distracted by market noise and have an emotional reaction to something that is going on. Interestingly, our survey of successful traders found that by and large they are generally not trading many positions at once. They focus their resources and attention on a small number of trades. Why? On an emotional level it's hard to manage multiple trades simultaneously. And a single emotional reaction to a bad trade has the potential to ruin several other trades that are actually winners; this happens because your logical mind has been commandeered by your emotions at that point. Part of good money management is knowing what your limits are in terms of the amount of time and energy you have to keep up on your trades. For the impulsive trader who trades too frequently, probably the best advice is to simply do less than you are inclined to do.

Remember how we said that personality traits are pervasive? That means that they generally span different areas of one's life and are not limited to one arena. So an impulsive person is generally going to be impulsive about many (maybe not all) things in life. Your typical impulsive person is going to find it just as hard to resist placing a trade too early as it is to resist eating that last piece of Black Forest chocolate cake in the refrigerator. Research shows that the best way to manage impulsivity (let's use the piece of chocolate cake to help us see this) is through (1) putting into place a system of checks, and (2) close monitoring. This applies to both Black Forest cake and trading the markets.

Remember reading about the story of Odysseus by Homer? Coming back from the Trojan wars, Odysseus ordered the members of his ship's crew to plug up their ears with wax and then had them tie him to his ship's mast in order to resist the Sirens' songs. He told the crew not to change the course of the ship under any circumstances, and he also gave clear instructions that they should not untie him. Odysseus had been warned, you see, about the Sirens by the enchantress Circe. But Odysseus wanted to hear the songs, so he took these extreme measures because he knew he was vulnerable. He had the foresight to appreciate his own weaknesses and temptations. He knew that in order to continue his long journey home, he needed to put in place a system that would prevent him from giving in. Indeed, if he had not been bound to the mast, he would have jumped overboard and drowned. From this ancient story of Homer's we see how the first step in gaining self-control is having insight into one's impulsive nature. Only then can one identify the correct steps needed to counteract one's impulsivity by employing various self-control strategies.

So, if you are high in N5, make sure you have a very clear written list of all the key variables (rules) that need to be checked off before making a move in the market. Make this list in advance, when your emotions are not running high, and then make sure you use it prior to every trade you make. By doing this, you can learn to take advantage of your impulsivity (which actually can be very useful when it comes to catching a quick move in the market).

By monitoring, which I said was needed in addition to checks, I mean turn to a trusted person to make sure you are following your checklist of variables. If you are very impulsive, do not take it upon yourself to make sure you are sticking to the plan!

A good analogy is a NASA rocket. You are the one who is sitting at your desk with a finger on the red button that ignites the main engines and propels the rocket upward into space. You are waiting, and you are eager. The weather forecaster says that there is a 10-minute window of opportunity for a successful launch (placing a trade in a market). At that point do you just go ahead and impulsively press the button and fire up the engines on this multi-million dollar toy?

No! You are going to go through a very rapid, but very comprehensive and orderly, checklist to make sure "all systems are go" prior to making that final and fateful decision. Just as NASA makes its checklists far in advance of launch time and practices them over and over in simulated launches, so should you. And just as NASA modifies its prelaunch checklists based on prior successes and failures, so should you. And just as at NASA, the guy with his finger hovering over the red launch button is not the same guy who is monitoring whether the checklist is being followed to a T, so too would it be ideal if you had someone else involved to make sure you are staying on task and not jumping the gun. At least until you train yourself well, look for a trading partner to help reinforce this type of prelaunch checklist behavior.

It is often thought that one big reason why professional investors and traders, in general, outperform the average individual investor is that they are required to operate under a strict set of institutional rules and regulations. These rules allow for greater control of emotional reactions. In contrast, the private trader is often, if not always, entirely on his or her own and has no set list of rules or procedures to follow. Of course, rogue institutional traders pop up from time to time in the news, professional traders who lose millions or even billions of dollars for their firms, usually by ignoring or finding ways around the institution's rules and allowing their emotions (greed or excitement) to go unbridled and unchecked.

Besides a checklist of rules to follow while trading, another key strategy you can employ to limit emotional reactivity (high neuroticism) is instilling "cool-off periods" into your trading behavior. In the heat of the moment, a trader can get very caught up in his market trades, so much so that the money behind his trades can start to appear abstract or unreal. Clicks of a computer mouse, ticks on a computer screen. The true value of what your trades represent can be lost in the hustle and bustle of it all. A cooling-off strategy allows you to step back, get a concrete grasp of what you are really risking and how much money is at stake, and visualize the potential consequences if things go wrong. You have to have a real sense of what the ramifications of your trading behavior could be. Things must be brought down from that abstract level and into very understandable and very real terms. Make sure to interject your cooling-off periods both before you place a trade (this may have to be very brief, perhaps just minutes, so you don't miss the trade altogether!), and immediately after the trade is executed or exited.

Keep in mind, too, that high N scores are not all bad! Bring back to your mind the image of the bell-shaped curve. Half the human population is going to come down on the neurotic side of the spectrum, albeit some much more so than others. Does that mean that half of us cannot be reasonably good traders in the market? Probably not. It turns out that it can also be advantageous to rate high on the N scale, as long as you recognize it and take full advantage of it. People who are high in N are, by definition, more emotionally sensitive. They are potentially more able to use this sensitivity to get a "gut feeling" about market trends. But they are going to have to put more effort and attention into controlling their emotions than those with lower N scores.

Meanwhile, for the person who is low in N, although his emotions are not getting in the way of intellectual mastery of the markets, he may miss out on experiencing certain subtle and intuitive emotional cues that can be helpful in deciphering when a good trade is going bad (or when a bad trade is starting to turn good). Being overly stoic and emotionally bland can be potentially a very dangerous thing. Remember, the best traders scored average in neuroticism overall. So if you are low in N, take note!

Back to fear and anxiety. Anxiety is often what keeps us in check (both in the markets and in life). If we were totally fearless, we would probably not make out too well. The fearless are the reckless.

Mental Edge Tips
- The best traders have low anxiety levels; this is true. But you need to understand your own strengths and weaknesses and then adapt to them.
- If you score low on the N scale, appreciate that you are someone who has a natural ability to manage trading problems by using cognitive processes such as problem solving and analysis and that your emotions are not often going to get in the way. You will not take wins or losses too personally. You likely still have emotional cues ("gut feelings"), but you experience them more weakly than those who are high in N, and hence it is going to be harder for you to pick up on them. So pay attention to that.
- Those high in N need to realize that you can be swept away by various negative emotions and that these feelings (anxiety, depression, guilt, self-deprecation) can easily interfere with the cognitive process of executing trades. For example, such a neurotic trader, after getting angry and frustrated over a losing trade, may decide to double the position size on the next trade in order to make the money back quickly. You may do so without thinking rationally about the size of your position, or even if there is really an indicator that a trade should be placed. It will be important for these traders to continually monitor their emotions (they should keep a diary or log—perhaps even use a mood rating scale on an hourly or daily basis) and avoid making decisions when emotions are still going strong. It would also be advisable that you allow time for these emotions to settle down and return to a baseline before entering the market again. Find ways to vent. Also, avoid trading systems that are very active in terms of frequency of trades, because you will need time to reset your emotions, and if your trading style is too active, this will not happen.

CHAPTER 15

CBT for Traders

Is it possible to actually treat neuroticism? As a physician and psychiatrist, I can tell you that, although we cannot change your personality much, high neuroticism (N) is very much indeed treatable. Sound like a contradiction? Let me try to be more clear. You cannot lower your innate propensity very much, but you can lower your emotional reactivity using various methods. It's kind of like telling a short-statured adult, "I can't make you grow any taller, but if you wear elevator shoes it will be almost the same thing, and you will be able to do things that tall people do." So we're talking more about temporary adaptation and accommodation, not permanent change.

A 1998 study by Knutson et al. in the *American Journal of Psychiatry*[1] demonstrated that even the administration of certain pills can appreciably change one's personality, notably by lowering his or her neuroticism. In the study, 26 healthy individuals were started on the SSRI antidepressant medication paroxetine (Paxil), while 25 control patients were given a placebo pill. As you may know, SSRIs are the most frequently used antidepressants today. SSRIs are approved by the FDA for treating people with serious primary mood disorders, such as major depression and various kinds of anxiety disorders, whereas SSRIs certainly have *not* been approved by the FDA for modulating personality.

But the research study showed that SSRIs could, indeed, be used to modulate personality. Healthy people (they were not suffering from any kind of mood disorder) who took paroxetine actually had a reduction in their levels of neuroticism after only four weeks (the NEO-AC was given before and after treatment). This finding stunned many psychiatrists and even made the mainstream media, as personality was previously thought to be largely stable and not something you could tweak with a pill!

However, there is no need even to take a pill to lower your N score. There is a plethora of other methods to help you reduce anxiety, including the kind of anxiety that is related to trading. Deep breathing exercises, self-hypnosis, bio-feedback, and guided imagery are all prime examples. But the most useful and effective form of treatment for individuals who are high in neuroticism is CBT (cognitive behavioral therapy).

CBT, as a therapy, is powerful, in that it has been substantially researched and has been proven to work. More important, it is based upon very solid psychological and physiological principals that can be demonstrated in both humans and lab animals. And the best part is that you can learn to train your brain in the same ways we train animals to behave or feel certain ways (through conditioned learning). The key is to rehearse, over and over, a desired set of positive emotions, thoughts, and behaviors during a period of time you are in a specific emotional state. It's the very best way to teach an old dog (you) new tricks (a healthy mental life).

If you feel that high neuroticism is severely affecting your financial well being or any other areas of your life (job, family, social life), you should really go see a CBT therapist for a full evaluation and professional treatment. But it is also possible to learn about and use some CBT techniques at home, and I would like to present you will a few tools that have benefited many successful traders. (Again, if you are "highly neurotic," hypersensitive, clinically depressed, or obsessive-compulsive, you truly need to be under the care of a CBT therapist who can help you work on your automatic thoughts and control them so that they don't take over your entire life.)

First, a little history lesson. In 1907 Dr. Sigmund Freud invited another physician, Dr. Alfred Adler, to help create and use psychological treatments for neuroses. Up until then there were only two (largely useless) treatment methods: (1) hypnosis and (2) dunking the neurotic person into a tub of ice-cold water.

Freud, Adler, and three of Freud's patients thus started the Wednesday Psychological Society, which went on to become the Viennese Psychoanalytic Society. Nine years later, Adler left Freud to form Individual Psychotherapy. This was the first holistic psychology, and for the past hundred years plus, it has been the most influential psychology school in the western world. By the 1960s, a psychotherapist named Aaron Beck, who at the time was still using the methods of free association and psychoanalysis, realized that many patients' strong emotions were tied directly to cognitions (thoughts) and that they did not bring these thoughts up during sessions of psychoanalysis. Beck went on to develop CBT, the paramount therapy in use today for most psychological conditions.

At its core, CBT recognizes that faulty thoughts or cognitions often lead to an adverse emotional response and that people tend to get stuck in patterns of having the same sorts of faulty thoughts and experiencing the same sorts of emotions over and over. The second part of CBT says that we enact a set of behaviors in response to the uncomfortable feelings that are provoked by the cognitive distortions. CBT works by reshaping the cognitive distortions (it changes the way you think and feel) and also by replacing the maladaptive behaviors with more healthy ones.

That all sounds like a bunch of psychobabble (even though it's not), so let's use a few examples to make it all more clear.

First, consider a dog phobia patient I once cared for and cured. This was a young woman in high school who, much earlier in life, had been severely attacked by a dog. She developed an extreme aversion to or fear of all dogs. Over the years she learned to avoid dogs. Anytime walking down the sidewalk if she were to see a dog approaching in front of her, she would cross over to the other side of the street or turn around and head the other way. Whenever visiting a house with a dog, she always made sure the dog was sequestered before entering.

This all came to a head one day when she was visiting a relative's house. The family dog, a totally harmless one I am told, was penned up in an upstairs bedroom. But somehow the dog escaped, pranced down the stairs, and headed right toward my dog phobic patient. Terrified, my patient reverted to her typical response to dogs: she began to turn and flee. Unfortunately, she turned right into a toddler and accidently knocked him to the ground, injuring the little tike.

It was at that point my patient and her family realized that she needed help for her anxiety problem concerning dogs. I turned to CBT. From a cognitive standpoint, we reformulated her beliefs about dogs ("Not all dogs are bad," and, "Not all barking means a dog is angry"). From a behavioral standpoint, I exposed the patient to the trigger, namely dogs, using titration and habituation. We started with pictures of dogs, then Youtube videos of dogs, then eventually graduated up to approaching live dogs. By the end of treatment, several months later, my patient had gotten to the point of being able to stand in the middle of a fenced-in dog park with 5 or 6 dogs running and barking around her. With enough exposure and mental restructuring, the fears went away.

But you didn't buy this book to be a better dog trainer. What is your anxiety when it comes to trading the markets? Let's say, for example, you place a buy trade in a market one morning. By the afternoon, you are happy, because you have some profits. You go to bed that night, feeling content in your ability to spot a winning entry point. But lo and behold, the next morning you wake up only to find that the market has taken a sudden downturn, and all of a sudden you realize you had forgotten to place a stop-loss order the day before. You just lost a hunk of money, all because of a rookie mistake, and you are not even a rookie. You start telling yourself, "You're so stupid, you idiot!" You not only berate yourself for forgetting to put in a stop, but you start telling yourself you are never going to become a successful trader at this rate, that you are destined to become a failure in the markets, no matter what. Sound familiar?

Soon all these self-deprecating ideas and words that you are hitting yourself on the head with will start making you feel a certain way (and it is not a positive feeling; trust me). You not only have the *idea* you are a loser, but you will soon start *feeling* like a loser. And before you know it, the next step is that you will engage in maladaptive behaviors of one form or another and actually start *behaving* like a loser. (I refer you back to Figure 1.1.)

Do you see the pattern? An event triggers you to have a distorted thought ("I am totally incompetent and stupid"). Your thought makes you feel a certain way (sad, angry, or what have you), and your feelings make you act in certain ways (self-destruction, regression, isolation, revenge).

It all started snowballing after you had an initial negative, and largely untrue, thought. But it's important to carefully examine the evidence. The truth is you had initially identified and placed a great trade! So clearly you are not stupid. The only reason it failed was that you were not careful in putting in a stop. You may have been a careless trader, but that does not make you an incompetent trader. Once the negative feelings set in, though, they can be hard to shake.

And it is those negative feelings (or any attempt to deal with, deny, or evade those feelings) that is going to interfere with your trading. Feeling low and irritable, are you going to get into an argument with someone you love, perhaps a spouse? Are you going to turn to alcohol to drown your tears away? Are you going to shut yourself away and stop socializing with your friends? Are you going to stop eating and exercising healthily? Or, much more subtly, on your next trade are you going to veer away from your tried, true, and proven trading methods (remember, it was a winning trade; you just forgot the stop!), all because you feel you are a loser?

Here is what to do. Use the four S's of CBT.

1. *Stop sign*—Whenever you sense a negative and untrue thought you don't want in your head, in your imagination hold up a huge red stop sign. Be creative. Perhaps your stop sign is held by a stern-faced crossing guard! Or perhaps think of a stop sign that is trimmed on all eight sides with giant, red blinking lights. Learn to recognize when you have an unwanted or untrue thought that is starting to form in your mind ("I am so stupid!"). At its earliest presence, go ahead and combat it with that stop sign in your mind. The more clear and specific your imaginary stop sign looks, the better. Some people even choose to make a physical stop sign, not just a mental one. Use the same stop sign each time. I know this sounds childishly simple and silly, but it really does work. There is good research behind it!

2. *Shout it out*—Shout at the negative thought. Scream at it, curse at it, yell at it with all your might (of course, not too loudly; we don't want the neighbors calling the police on you!) until you can sense that the unwanted thought is leaving your mind. How is this going to possibly

change anything, you may be wondering? Well, the nice thing about the human mind is that it basically cannot contain more than a single conscious thought at any one time. Treat the unwanted thought as an intruder in your mind, someone you *do not* want in there! Get angry at it! Banish it!

3. *Substitute*—Have handy a sentence or thought to put in the place of the unwanted thought. Make it something strong, something positive, and something you really want to believe! Some people carry such positive or self-encouraging thoughts with them on 3-inch × 5-inch note cards. Or type it up, print it out, and place it directly above your computer monitor. An example substitution thought might be: "I am a capable trader, and I am learning from my mistakes!"

4. *Sustain*—Keep at it. As you kick the unwanted thought out the front door, it will turn around and try to sneak in a window or down the chimney! *Don't let it!* Also, reflect on what happened. Is it possible you created the unwanted thought for a reason? Psychology of use says you think all your thoughts (even the ones you don't want) in order to get something from them! In our example above, the reason you are telling yourself, "I am incompetent and stupid" is really because you were careless and forgot to put a stop order in. So realistically you need to recognize the mistake you made for what it is and why it happened (in this case it was due to carelessness, but not stupidity). Identifying and appreciating the true situation, that you are actually very smart but at times careless, you can now move on to rectify the problem, that is, next time you will be more careful and place that stop!

Keep repeating the four Ss until you find yourself in charge of the thought you don't want. As you become more comfortable with this, you'll find you are more in control of your whole mind and also of your negative feelings. Again, the point is to catch yourself with a negative thought *before* it creates negative feelings and negative behaviors. By using this simple four-step approach faithfully, you will find you have much more control over your unwelcome and disturbing thoughts and emotions, and you will become a better trader because of it!

One common mistake that trader's frequently make is to concurrently mix trading with emotional processing. They may try analyzing or dealing with their emotions right in the midst of active trading. This is never a wise thing. Trading takes a lot of concentration and mental wherewithal. So does CBT. Bottom line: Don't attempt "self-talk" or CBT techniques while you are immersed in the markets. When trading, stay focused to what is on your screen, indicators that will be important to you, and so on. Save your CBT, deep breathing exercises, and whatnot for when you can really devote yourself to it (before trades, after trades, or when you are in a trade, but can turn away from it for a while).

If you notice you are getting very anxious while trading, step away from your screen long enough to appreciate what is making you anxious. You probably don't want to be making decisions blindly based on fears anyway. Again, don't mix self-help strategies and trading—you will fail at both.

You can even take CBT to a deeper and more powerful level if you so choose. Let's look at a more advanced CBT technique. Let's say that you have tremendous anxiety over when to exit trades. Your current (and unhealthy) routine and predictable behavior is to exit a winning trade too early, resulting in reduced profits and a sense of self-failure. Your desired new behavior is to hold onto winning trades longer (ideally up to the point of maximum profit, of course).

The first step in changing your behavior is to choose a strenuous endurance activity you enjoy and are reasonably good at. This could be running, swimming, biking, jump roping, or what have you. Whatever the activity, you are going to tether it to the desired goal, and then condition yourself to the response.

To do this, set aside a 30-minute block of time every day to work exclusively on this task. Each time, as you gradually start to engage in the chosen physical activity (let's say running on a treadmill), start to become aware of your body's physical response (heart rate goes up, breathing faster, sweating, more alert). Simultaneously, begin mentally rehearsing the desired behavior or feeling in your mind's eye. Imagine yourself, in this example, holding onto your winning trades longer. As you are jogging along, envision yourself seated at your trading desk in front of the computer monitor you usually use. Visualize trades on your monitor and what it feels like to hold onto the trades. Imagine in your mind's eye that the market is tempting you to exit your position—but resist the urge! What does it feel like? Imagine how happy, content, and masterful you feel as you continue to rack up profits in the face of anxiety that tells you to exit now. Keep holding onto your position; resist the temptation to take your profits early. Persist. Again, you are imagining all of this while engaged in your chosen physical activity (running on the treadmill).With frequent repetition of this very simple exercise, your brain will begin to associate the desired goal with your body's alert, energized, and pumped-up state. This is conditioning. Keep conditioning yourself with the same goal connected to the same stimulus (activity). Do not alter or deviate from the routine.

Eventually, after your brain is fully conditioned, you will arrive at a point where, just by engaging in the stimulating activity (running), your brain will automatically kick in to the desired framework (positive emotions, confidence, a sense of mastery) that will help you produce the desired effect(s). You will not even have to remind yourself to think about the desired feeling or behavior, because it is now a habit that comes naturally.

Next, with your brain fully primed, use the same exercise (running on the treadmill) immediately before you begin a trading session. Do you see what you are doing here? You are programming your mind to feel and react a certain way and then calling on it when needed. Give yourself "booster shots" during trading breaks. Every time you engage in the activity, you will trigger your brain to react in the way you have trained it to. In this example, you will now find it much easier to tolerate the anxiety associated with holding onto winning trades until the market reaches your target exit point.

For those of you who are skeptical about using such easy and cheap (actually, free) CBT methods to lower your neuroticism, I would urge you to consider these data. The proof of the pudding is in the eating. In 1989, a meta-analysis was done by a researcher in Australia looking at what types of therapies were most effective in modifying neuroticism. (A meta-analysis, by the way, is a study which combines the results of many other studies into one large, mega research project. By combining the results of lots of studies you can be more confident in the results.)

The results of this study (Jorm, *Australian and New Zealand Journal of Psychiatry*[2]) showed that "rational-emotive and related therapies" were far and away the most effective method of reducing neuroticism. "Rational-emotive therapy" is the precursor of what today we refer to as CBT. In fact, the study showed that all the other therapy methods (including meditation, stress inoculation, muscle relaxation, group therapy, study skills trading, and anxiety management training) were really about as effective as placebo in reducing neuroticism, while rational-emotive therapy was three times more effective than placebo. Also, the effects of this therapy were lasting; even a year after treatment study participant's retained their lower neuroticism levels.

Back to medications. In 2009 a second study (Tang, *Archives of General Psychiatry*[3]) showed that SSRI drugs are helpful in reducing neuroticism (similar to the first study I cited in this chapter). However, Tang's study also showed that CBT was able to reduce neuroticism (though not as effectively as the drug). In 2010 an article by Glinski[4] in the journal *Behavior Change* added more weight, as she too showed, "Treatment (with CBT) was associated with significant reductions in neuroticism."

The field of cognitive behavioral therapy continues to evolve and be better defined by clinical research. Today, in 2012, one exciting and promising cutting edge of CBT is a specific subtype of therapy called cognitive bias modification (CBM). CBM, developed primarily by reputable psychologists at Brown University, is a therapy that is delivered entirely via computer software and has been shown in multiple small clinical trials to be a very good potential treatment for combating anxiety (recall that top market traders have low trait anxiety levels). Although the trials have been limited in scope and size and much more needs to be elucidated, CBM appears to be as effective as in-person therapy or drugs for treating anxiety.

CBM consists of performing very simple exercises several times per week for four to six weeks, using a computer program that is designed to teach and train the brain to cope better with anxiety. The idea of computer-based therapy is certainly controversial. Many psychotherapists of course are opposed to the idea, primarily over fear that clients would be able to manage and temper their anxiety entirely from the comforts of home—without the need of a pricey therapist. Others are skeptical that something as simple as a computer program could help people substantially lower anxiety. Psychologists and psychiatrists in general consider anxiety (both from primary mental disorders and neurotic personalities) one of the hardest mental symptoms to treat or manage—much harder than depression, for instance. The idea that a computer program can be as effective as psychotropic medications or intense psychotherapy in controlling anxiety just doesn't compute for some, but the data are starting to show that it just might be!

CBM software uses an "attention" technique, which trains people to ignore an anxiety-provoking cue and to instead complete a simple task. Here's a simple example: On a split computer screen, research subjects are simultaneously shown pictures of both a disgusted or frightening human face and a neutral human face. Which face appears on which side of the screen is random, and over an hour or so about a thousand of these split screen images show up in a rapid succession. For each screen shot shown to the research subject, one of the two faces is quickly replaced with a letter (either an E or an F), while the other face remains on the screen. The incredibly simple task given to the research subjects is to report which letter pops up on the screen each time, simply by clicking either the E of F on the keyboard. Two groups of people are tested: a therapy group and a placebo group. For those receiving the active CBM therapy, the neutral appearing face is always the one replaced by a letter and the disgusted face always remains on the computer screen. In this manner, the research subjects are forced (trained) to divert their attention away from the anxiety-provoking face, so they can complete the simple task. Meanwhile, for the placebo group, either of the two faces has an equal chance of being replaced by the letter E or F.

In a nutshell, you are training your brain to make cognitive decisions (figuring out which letter is being presented to you) in the face of a noxious and anxiety-provoking stimulus. Sound too easy and too good to be true? Well the data so far show that the CBM treatment substantially and even dramatically lowers anxiety following four to six weeks in the treatment group, and not at all in the placebo group. CBM still needs to be proven in larger trials with longer follow-up times, but so far, this therapy appears to be very promising as a way to effectively reduce anxiety. It has started to receive attention in popular media, including *The Economist*, and

I think you will be hearing much more about the burgeoning field of CBM. And remember, our research shows that the best traders are those who are low in trait-anxiety on the NEO-AC. So, if there is a way to program your brain to be less anxious, it may very well help your trade results!

Mental Edge Tips
- CBT is not new. But there is a revolutionary concept that is coming about, that personality traits such as neuroticism can be modified with therapy, or even pills. The idea "once a neurotic always a neurotic" is being proven false, or at least will need to be modified, because it now appears that CBT does more than just change your perceptions, feeling, and behaviors. It actually tempers your underlying temperamental traits, so that when a stressful situation arises, you will be more ready to confront it.
- Although there has been absolutely no research specifically looking at reducing neuroticism in investors or traders using CBT or CBM methods, look for this in the near future. In the meantime, you will likely benefit from employing these strategies, if anxiety is a major hindrance in your trading.

CHAPTER 16

Risk Aversion and Trading

Risk aversion (along with its opposite, risk propensity) is a complex concept, in either psychology or finance. It can be either very fun or very dull to learn about. Go ahead and Google, "Arrow-Pratt Measure of Risk Aversion," if you want a very dry, impractical, and (at least for your purposes) useless model of risk aversion.

In fact, we all intuitively know what risk aversion means. It refers to the process of making decisions after carefully weighing the risks and benefits associated with the choice. On one end of the spectrum, one person may need to be offered a huge reward to balance even the slightest amount of risk (this is somebody who is highly risk averse). Another person may take incredibly great risks in the hope of only a minimal benefit (a person with very low risk aversion). Most of us fall somewhere in between on the spectrum of risk aversion.

But risk aversion is actually a bit more complex than that. When it comes to risk-taking and the markets, there are two main forces (rewards) at play. First, there is the potential reward of making a monetary profit. Compared to safer (less volatile and less leveraged) financial investments, the futures markets offer speculators the chance to take greater risks in order to satisfy their greed (let's call it what it is) for money and the nice things money can provide (better food, house, car, clothing, vacations, college education for children). The other potential "reward" in market trading is sensation-seeking: the thrill and excitement that trading itself can offer. These two rewards, making money and excitement-seeking, are not mutually exclusive. In and of themselves they are not necessarily bad. Although money is "the root of all evil," it can also be the root of a lot of goodness.

These two basic rewards have been programmed into our genes and have been hardwired into our brains. After all, humans are a risk-taking species by nature. Our ancient ancestors originated in East Africa, and within a span of only 100,000 years (which, relatively speaking, is but a blink of the eye in terms of life on this planet) spread over the entire globe. How were our ancestors able to do it? Their "explorativeness" and willingness to take risks is likely one of the keys to the survival and thriving success of our species.

When you stop and think about it, the hunting of large and dangerous game by prehistoric men was a very risky endeavor. In comparison to their prey, our ancestors were small, slow, and had no built-in armor (tusks, thick skin, or the like) or other protective mechanisms (wings to fly away when things got dicey). Compared to market traders sitting behind their computer monitors, these were the real risk-takers! Certainly the huge success and globalization of the human species depended upon these hunters being smart and creative, which was determined by the superior size of their cerebral cortexes. But it still required a lot of risk-taking to make it work. The risks these ancient ancestors took were driven by a desire (greed) for a bigger hunk of meat, but equally so this dangerous hunting probably also provided a sense of thrill and excitement ("the chase," "the adrenaline rush"). If there were no thrill or rush to the hunt, it's possible our ancestors may have been satisfied with a life of gathering and eating fruits, nuts, and berries (like most other primates).

When we modern humans make financial or investment decisions and contemplate our own willingness to take on risk, we need to be aware that we do this both out of our propensity for greed *and* because we like the thrill or the rush of trading. (It's very akin to sexual intimacy. If there were no thrill or rush, many humans might be less willing to take on the risk of being parents.) Again, it is built into us, and the two rewards (greed and thrill) are closely tied together.

That said, not everyone is amenable to the same degree of risk-taking. Risk-taking is a trait, and there is a wide variability (spectrum or dimension) to the extent people take risks. Futures traders clearly are, relatively speaking, financial risk-takers. They are willing to take longer odds in the hope of making bigger gains. More risk-averse investors, meanwhile, likely have all of their investments in mutual funds or exchange traded funds. The *very* risk-averse investor, of course, plops all of his or her money into a FDIC-insured savings accounts that pays 1 or 2 percent annual interest.

Further, some of us trade mostly for the prospect of making money (and the things money provides) and don't get as much of a "high" from trading, while others primarily trade the markets because they get their kicks from the actual trading. Those in this second group are typically the unsuccessful traders and the people who develop addictions to trading the markets. (See Chapter 23 for more on the topic of addictions.)

Most of us probably take risks in trading because of a combination of the two rewards: It's a chance to make money quickly, and there is some excitement associated with it. But be sure of this: Your average *successful* futures trader is *not* an extreme risk taker. The extreme risk taker is the person who gambles his last thin dime in Las Vegas at the roulette wheel, hoping and praying for a miracle.

Think about it: Markets can only go in one of three directions; they can go up, go down, or stay relatively flat. Compare that to how many different slots a roulette ball could land in (there are 38 slots on the American roulette wheel). And while the final outcome of the ball in the roulette wheel depends entirely on Lady Luck, trading the markets actually involves an incredible amount of knowledge, experience, insight, computational ability, planning, pattern recognition and judgment—along with a healthy portion of luck. Genuine market traders are speculators, not gamblers.

The word speculate comes from the Latin word *speculatus*, meaning "to spy out" and "to examine." Traders are speculators in the sense that they are risk-takers, but they base their decisions on a lot of research, hard work, insight, and eventual understanding of various forces that drive the markets up and down.

There is no one facet on the NEO-AC that corresponds best to risk aversion versus risk-taking. Rather, research shows risk aversion can best be understood using a composite of several of the personality traits. A 2008 study[1] published in *Financial Services Review* by Cliff Mayfield et al., for instance, found that there is a significant negative correlation between both openness (O) and extraversion (E) and investment-specific risk aversion. That is, people who are high in O and/or high in E are more likely to take risks with investments than people low in O and E. The study also found that personal characteristics influence investors' perception of risk, and that their perception of risk was determining their investing behavior. As an example, they found that individuals who are more open to new experiences (high in O) tend to engage in long-term investing. However, one major shortcoming of this article was that it did not confirm that this kind of behavior was actually advantageous; that is, it did not confirm that people high in O actually are more successful in their investments by using a longer-term strategy.

A very large and detailed study[2] of risk propensity was done by Nigel Nicholson and others at the London School of Business. Using NEO-AC data on 2,041 British financial traders (key point: they were not necessarily successful investors), risk aversion was measured across six different decision domains:

1. Recreational risks (rock-climbing, scuba diving)
2. Health risks (smoking, poor diet, excessive alcohol consumption)
3. Career risks (quitting a job without another to go to)
4. Financial risks (risky investments, gambling)
5. Safety risks (fast driving, motorcycling without a helmet)
6. Social risks (standing for election, publicly challenging a rule or decision)

This study found that a strong Big Five personality pattern emerges for people who are risk takers across all six of these domains: They are high in both E and O and low in N, A, and C. The authors of the study also found, however, that risk-taking is not quite the same across all six decision domains. As an example, there are big reductions over a person's lifetime in recreational, health, and safety risk-taking behaviors, while there are relatively small reductions or even no changes in career, financial, or social risk-taking behaviors across one's lifetime. Although the researchers did not speculate on the reason for this discrepancy in risky behaviors, I would propose that it relates to the underlying *reason* for the risky

behaviors. Safety risks, such as racing a motorcycle down the freeway, are more about getting the adrenaline rush going, and there
is little other gain or motivation for it. Social and financial risks,
on the other hand, involve taking the specified risk with the hope
and knowledge that something good and tangible will come of it,
something that will make the risk worthwhile.

But we are especially interested in knowing if there is a identifiable personality profile for people who take risks more for the
thrill of it versus people who take risks more because they are hoping to get something out of it (greed). Further, is there a different
personality profile for traders who go on to develop an addiction to
trading compared to people who do not?

On the facet level, Nicholson found that high E5 (excitement-
seeking) and high O6 (openness to values) were the greatest pre-
dictors of risk-taking in all six of the decision domains as well as
in overall risk-taking. Nicholson theorized that high E (especially
excitement seeking) and high O supply the "motivational force" for
people to take risks, while low N and low A insulate risk takers from
concern over negative consequences, and low C lowers the cognitive barriers to taking risks. Nicholson assumes that people low in
C will attempt to secure various benefits (monetary or otherwise)
by taking risks compared to those high in C, who will pursue the
same benefits through disciplined striving, rather than risk-taking.

So let's see how the investors in Nicholson's study stack up
against our top-notch futures traders in Table 16.1.

TABLE 16.1

Comparison of Risk-Taking Traits in Investors at Large Versus Our
Top-Notch Traders

	Nicholson's Study of Investors at Large	Top-Notch Traders
N	Low	Average
E	High	Average
O	High	Average
A	Low	Average
C	Low	Average
E5 (excitement-seeking)	High	Average
O6 (openness to values)	High	Average

So what's going on here? Is it that futures traders don't take risks? Not likely. Or is it that *successful* futures traders, that is, those we tested, are not high-risk individuals? The fact that a high E5 (excitement-seeking) was the most important facet score in determining risk-taking behavior in Nicholson's study, whereas our cohort of successful futures traders had an average E5 score, says a lot. It tells me that the thrill factor, as a reason for trading, is less important to the successful trader than it is to the average investor. Monetary rewards and likely other psychological rewards and benefits are driving the successful traders. Also, I think that our successful futures traders are not transsituational risk-takers.

Further, the average N and A scores support the notion that our successful traders are better equipped compared to average traders, who have low N and A, to be aware of potential negative consequences associated with risk taking. Those who are low in certain N and A facets don't possess fear. Fear is good. It's healthy. Not too much, of course, just enough fear to keep you out of harm's way. And the successful traders have that.

Don't confuse fear with anxiety here. When I say successful traders have a healthy dose of fear, I am referring to their C1 facet scores, which are discussed in the next chapter.

Also, the average C score of the successful trader indicates that he or she remains disciplined and works hard and diligently at this very risky endeavor. He or she applies controlled efforts to master the art of trading. Conversely, people with low overall C are more susceptible to "get rich quick" behaviors; that is, they attempt to cut corners, find the easy way instead of the right way, and so forth.

Further interesting comparisons can be made with the personality traits of problem gamblers, a topic of numerous research studies. (See Table 16.2.) You will note that, like the risk takers in Nicholson's study of investors at large, problem gamblers have low A and low C, but they are high N (especially impulsivity, N5).

Although the column in Table 16.2 under "Top-Notch Futures Traders" reads "average" right on down the line, it is important to keep in mind that there is a degree of variability in some of the facets, and after detailed interviewing with these traders, some patterns emerged. For example, there is great deal of variability in the O4, O5, and O6 scores of successful traders, and from our discussions

TABLE 16.2

Personality Comparisons Between Investors at Large, Successful
Futures Traders, and Problem Gamblers

	Study of Investors at Large	Top-Notch Futures Traders	Problem Gamblers
Total N	Low	Average	High
Total E	High	Average	Average
Total O	High	Average	Average
Total A	Low	Average	Low
Total C	Low	Average	Low
E5 (excitement-seeking)	High	Average	Average
O6 (openness to values)	High	Average	Average

with these traders a trend seems to emerge. Traders who are high
in O5 (ideas) or O6 (values) seem to be especially motivated to get
involved in futures trading, not for a rush or thrill, but for a deeper
psychological need. That is, they truly enjoy the challenge of learning and mastering something very difficult. Don't get me wrong,
the primary reason they are doing it is to make money (greed). But
the pursuit of mastery is also very tempting and very rewarding to
them as well.

Interestingly, our discussions with traders find that the O4
(actions) facet of the NEO-AC seems to measure a trader's level of
greed pretty well. O4 is a barometer, not just for the psychological
greed or lust of wealth, but also for the actual decision to pursue it.
Those who trade first and foremost to find "a bigger hunk of meat"
have higher O4 scores. They are willing to go out on a limb (the action)
and do something they have never done before in order to haul in a
big financial reward. They climb out on the limb, not because of the
thrill in tempting the branch to see if it will bear their weight, but
because they are in pursuit of some treasured fruit they hope will
be found growing at the end of the limb. They take the risk *despite*
the possibility that the branch may break, not because of it. (Keep in
mind that for many, if not most, people there are components of both
thrill and greed in their risk-taking behaviors. So relatively speaking, "high O4" traders are greedier and less thrill-seeking.)

We already described in detail how greed can be a good thing and how it is even an innate quality that is built into the human species. However, too much of anything (yes, even oxygen) can be bad and potentially lethal. Life and successful living is all about balance. There is a tendency for many aspiring futures traders to be high in O4/greed. My father's way of putting it is, "Traders have bigger greed glands than others."

Being excessively greedy can clearly be a very unhealthy thing. Going too far out on too thin a limb in search of riper fruit can be very hazardous to your health. While we all have some degree of greed, we need to learn to temper our greed with an appreciation for what we have in our lives. If this greed is not controlled or managed properly, it will surely lead to a trader's downfall. It is important to recognize and learn to live with your greed, and neither deny it nor exploit it. Our successful traders who are high in O4 have learned to do that. We'll get back to this in a moment.

Since most legitimate futures traders are not trading the markets purely to get a rush (the way someone gets a rush from driving fast when there is no need or benefit to doing so), the rest of this chapter will discuss risk-taking from the perspective of how high someone scores on the facets O4 to O6. Keep in mind, though, that the other risk-aversion facets, especially E5, can be equally wrapped up in how risky your trading habits may be or become. In general, we have found that the higher your O4, O5, and O6 scores, the less risk averse you are (more willing to take risks), while, conversely, someone with very low O4 to O6 scores is someone who is very risk averse (tends to avoid taking risks). Interestingly, we found successful futures traders all along this spectrum, from high to low risk aversion.

A risk-averse market trader (lower O4 to O6) is going to have difficulty tolerating the concept of larger losses. This person is, from a personality standpoint, much more suited to smaller, more frequent and more controlled trades. Trading in smaller time frames is also more appropriate for these traders, as they are not people who are looking for big and protracted market runs. They are looking to pinpoint the smaller market moves that come and go more frequently. Using smaller time frames allows such a trader to control risk with the holding period.

An effective strategy for these traders is to use very tight stops. That is to say, these are people who will benefit from very close money management. They should more frequently monitor how the market is doing so that they can adjust their stops and positions as needed. These are not people who should enter a position and then go on a long vacation to a remote tropical island where they will have no ability to monitor and manage their risks.

A good analogy here is surfing. Risk-averse traders are those surfers who are looking for the more frequent and reliable, albeit smaller, wave breaks. At the end of the surfing day, they would rather have mounted and ridden many small or medium-sized waves as opposed to waiting for one giant wave.

In comparison, low risk-averse traders (high O4 to O6) hope to catch the mammoth waves; they are more than happy to let the routine, mundane (to them) waves go by as they seek out that monster ride. They have a tolerance for taking such risks.

If you are a relatively risk-adverse market trader, as you are paddling out to where the waves are breaking, pay close attention to where and how the swells are forming (that is, how the markets are moving). Only stand up on your surfboard and ride those waves that you can see and feel are going to be a size to your liking. If you see a potentially huge wave forming or great instability developing in the markets, be careful not to be tricked into riding it (particularly if you also scored high in N5—impulsivity!), as your level of risk aversion is likely ill-prepared for such a ride.

No matter how tempting it looks, it's probably best if you keep your tummy and head flat on your surfboard and let that giant wave go right on by you. Let the big-wave surfers get their kicks on those giant 30-foot swells—and potentially crash spectacularly into the reef and rocks. Reassure yourself that surely there will be plenty more 7-foot waves yet to come that are more your style and more to your liking. The risk-averse traders are going to be challenged during periods of high market volatility, and it is best for them to stay on the sidelines during those times.

A trader who is less risk averse (high O4 to O6), on the other hand, is someone who is drawn to the possibility of larger wins, with the full understanding that there could be greater drawdowns, bumps, and bruises along the way. They are willing to take big risks in hopes of cashing in on big returns. These traders enjoy the stimulation and challenge of taking bigger risks: They seek them out and even thrive on them!

These are the surfers who, with glee, head to the North Shore of Oahu in late December because they know that's when and where the big waves are rolling in! They are better suited for taking on larger positions (large relative to the size of their own investment portfolio, not necessarily large in comparison to that of another trader). Trading too small a position (small waves) has the potential to lull the risk-taking trader to sleep. She may lose focus and may potentially make bad decisions simply because she is not paying close enough attention to her positions There is not enough at stake for her to really take interest—at least not until she realizes the trade has gone bust.

Bigger risk-takers are also better at holding onto their positions for longer periods of times. They are able to tolerate the intra-trade instability that is sure to be present. Big bull and bear moves in the market are never arrows that go straight up or straight down. High O4 to O6 traders are better able to ride out the instability and ups and downs that comprise the overall market swing. Their stops can and should be looser.

Risk-taking traders (and especially those who are also high on the N5, impulsivity, scale), should take great care not to enter the market during a period of low volatility. If there are no huge swells forming right now, don't be tempted to ride the smaller waves just to pass the time or because you are bored. If you do fall into this trap, you can be sure the next big market move is going to start forming at a time when you are not ready to put your full concentration on it. Or you may miss it outright, simply because the small wave distracted you from seeing the big one that is forming. Keep in mind, too, that different markets are historically more prone to volatility than others. Depending on your risk-aversion score, you may fair better in one market over another. Find a surfing location that matches your level of risk aversion.

If you are high in O (again, especially O4 to O6), high in E5 (excitement seeking), as well as high in N, you need to especially watch out for the following common personality trap. Your penchant for excitement and thrills may entice you to make a trade, not because it is the wise thing to do, but because you are looking for a way to instill some action or stimulation in your life. Then, once realizing it was a mistake and that you are in over your head, you panic. Your neuroticism kicks in after one or several losing, high-risk trades. Now, not for excitement seeking, but purely out of anger, anxiety, guilt, depression, or impulsiveness, you make yet another bad decision, which only compounds your loses.

Here's one final learning point about risk aversion. While innate personality has a lot to do with a person's risk aversion or risk-taking behavior, it likely is not the whole story. In 2006 researchers at University Hospital Zurich's Key Brain-Mind Research Center demonstrated[3] that risk-taking can potentially be a modifiable behavior. They used low-frequency, repetitive transcranial magnetic stimulation (TMS) to transiently disrupt the function of a part of the brain's cortex called the dorsolateral prefrontal cortex (DLPFC) in a group of normal people. They then applied a well known gambling paradigm that provides a measure of decision making under risk. Individuals displayed significantly riskier decision making after disruption of the right, but not the left, DLPFC. These findings suggest that the right DLPFC plays a crucial role in the suppression of superficially seductive options and risk taking. So it appears that this fundamental human capacity, risk taking, can actually be manipulated in normal subjects through cortical stimulation.

Why is this research result potentially important for you? After all, although TMS has been approved by the FDA for the treatment of refractory depression and other mood disorders, it is unlikely that most market traders will ever have their right DLPFC stimulated by a giant magnet. The message to take away is that risk aversion may not be as immutable as was once thought. In fact, I am sure we all know people (if not ourselves) who took bigger risks in their early adult years, only to become more risk-averse as they grew older.

Not only that, but there is also now research showing that risk-aversion behavior can actually change during cyclical patterns in the market. For example, a 2009 research study[4] by Daniel Smith and Robert Whitelaw gave us for the first time hard evidence that levels of risk aversion in investors increase during times of economic contractions. This makes intuitive and theoretical sense. (Yet another body of research shows that an individual's own personal wealth, regardless of size, will not change his level of risk aversion—a rich investor's risk aversion will not increase or decrease if he loses his personal fortune.)

The point is, risk aversion is not necessarily static, and it is important to monitor one's own level of risk aversion and be aware that it may change over time or during certain market conditions. If and when your level of risk aversion changes, you should adapt your market strategies accordingly.

Mental Edge Tips
- Openness facets O4, O5, and O6 correspond well to risk aversion, especially the greed component of it.
- You can be a successful market trader regardless of whether your O facets are high or low. The key is that you need to identify trading strategies that match your level of risk aversion. Successful traders look for market volatility that matches their personalities.
- Expected duration of trade, placing appropriate stops, and relative size of trades to one's overall portfolio are also crucial keys to matching risk aversion to trading.

CHAPTER 17

Conscientiousness and Trading

In general, the conscientiousness (C) factor of personality rates a person's degree of self-control, perseverance, and striving for achievement. Those who have an overall high C score are good rule followers. This is particularly true for those high in facets C2 (order) and C3 (dutifulness). If this is you, you will do well trading mechanical systems. Systems trading is rule-based; the trading system dictates which trades to make and when. System trading decisions are absolute (if the criteria are met, the trade is made no matter what) and do not offer you the opportunity to decline to make a trade based upon your own discretion. For example, if a system trader reviews her charts and finds that her trading system's requirements for a trade have been met, she will make the trade without any further decision-making process (that is, regardless of whether she liked the price, if she has a "gut feeling," or whatnot).

As system trading decisions are absolute, system trading is perfectly suitable for fully automated trading. Once a computer program has been developed to recognize when a trading system's requirements have been met, the program can be designed so that it executes the trade (including the entry, management, and exit) without any (or minimal) involvement of the trader. There are various trading technologies and charting software programs on the market that provide the ability for such automated trading, (VisualStation from TickCom, for example).

The trend that we found in all of our top-notch traders was this: High C, and especially high C2/order, was associated with systems trading (see Chapter 24 on KD Angle). Someone high in C2 feels he has to stick to his formula and a well-defined set of rules. And for him, this works. However (as we will especially see later on, in the chapter about my dad's personality), traders with lower total C or C2 scores cannot stick to systems, and would probably even feel uncomfortable just reading the chapter on KD!!

Of course no trading system is totally automated. For instance, it is always up to the trader which system she is going to follow, in which market, and so forth. And it would not be surprising if an impulsive (high N5) system-based trader had a tendency to break the rules of the system she is trying to follow. But in general, we can think of high-C people as being well suited for systems trading.

Those who are low in C, especially in C2 or C3, will feel confined by and have trouble following the rules of mechanical trading systems. (Note: If you are low in the C2 or C3 facets and are also low in O, this is even more true.)

If your C scores are low, you are probably going to have more success trading discretionarily. Discretionary trading is decision-based trading: The trader ultimately decides which trades to make and when. The discretionary trader makes the best decision he can, based upon all of the information available at the time. A discretionary trader may still, in some ways, follow a trading system with clearly defined trading rules, but in the end he will use his own discretion (hence the name, discretionary trading) to decide whether or not to actually make each trade. His discretion always can and will trump the trading system. For example, a discretionary trader might review his charts and find that all of the criteria for a trade have been met, but decline to make the trade simply because he believes that the price is too high, the market is too volatile at the moment, or whatnot.

Both discretionary trading and mechanical or system trading have the potential to be equally profitable. There are fabulously successful systems traders, and there are just as many very successful discretionary traders. From our research, the decision about which trading style to adopt should be based upon the personality of the trader.

Some traders are intuitively and in some cases are instantly able to recognize which type of trading is more suitable for them. Perhaps they have especially good insight into their personalities, perhaps one form of trading "just feels right" to them, or perhaps by a stroke of luck they get started with the right style of trading and are never even exposed to the other. Meanwhile, other traders may struggle with deciding whether they should follow systems or discretionary methods, and it is for these traders that NEO-AC testing can be especially helpful. But this revelation is most critical for the poor and unfortunate market trader who has been stuck trying to trade using one form or the other (systems or discretionary) and has lost money time and again, never realizing that his innate personality simply does not match the style of trading he has adopted and persevered with for so long, without trying the other flavor of trading.

Pure discretionary trading is most compatible with traders who want to be in personal control of every trading decision (the entry, every aspect of the management, and the exit). Pure discretionary traders often feel uncomfortable and anxious when they think about giving complete control of their trading to a computer program. And remember from our earlier discussion, excess anxiety usually does not parlay into successful trading; discretionary traders often have personal backgrounds in artistic or visual endeavors, such as painting, writing, and gardening, and hence they will often also score high on facets O1 and O2: fantasy and aesthetics.

Match your trading style to your personality. The more conscientious you are, the more you will want to employ a style that is based on rules and is detail-oriented. For those lower in conscientiousness, trying to trade in such a highly structured manner will only lead to frustration and likely failure. Such a trader will likely do far better with "big picture trades"—trades that do not follow detailed rules, formulas or analysis, but rather require interpretation and creativity

If your C score (and especially facets C2 and C3) is neither high nor low, but average, then what? This is when blending trading styles might be most fruitful. For example, it is certainly possible to be a discretionary trader who uses some system trading. It is far more difficult to be a true system trader who uses discretionary trading. For example, a discretionary trader may follow a trading system for his entries and take every trade that the system identifies, but then manage and exit trades using personal discretion. A purist system trader does not have this option, because he must follow his trading system exactly. Once a system trader deviates from the hard and fast rules of his trading system, by definition he has become a discretionary trader.

Interestingly, Lo, Repin, and Steenbarger's research[1] on personality and successful trading found that high C resulted in more profits in trading. Keep in mind that this research was different from ours. They studied the personalities of both successful and unsuccessful traders, while we only studied the personalities of the very most successful traders. When interviewing the subjects in his study, Steenbarger found that half of the successful traders reported using mechanical systems. The other half all reported that, although they did not use systems per se, they did base their trades on specific patterns that they had carefully investigated. Meanwhile, of the less profitable traders in Steenbarger's study, none were mechanical traders, and none were grounded in pattern research.

Does this evidence imply that all traders should either follow systems or use careful pattern recognition? At the very least, it would seem to suggest that this is a good starting point for many, especially those high in C. But this thinking is actually contradicted by our own research, which shows that there are very successful traders who are average or even a bit low in C, and who do not follow specific systems. In fact, this subset of traders recognizes that they fair worse when trying to stick to systems.

The facet C1 (competence) also deserves extra attention in our critique of conscientiousness. The term competence somewhat distorts what C1 is all about. Scoring high in C1 does not mean you are a more competent trader. Think of C1 more in terms of confidence. Confidence, clearly, is a good thing. But we all know that having either too much or too little confidence can be a big problem when it comes to trading—or to life in general.

Traders who score very high in C1, on the other hand, need to be aware that they are prone to believing too much in themselves, their skill, their knowledge, or the system they created. Excess confidence that is not grounded in reality can be disastrous. It typically leads to inadequate money management and the outright ignoring of very real potential risks. Simply put, overconfident traders tend to deceive themselves into thinking that they are smarter and more in control of things than they really are.

They start to think they are immune to rookie mistakes. They think they have stumbled onto a trading pattern or system that is "flawless" and outperforms anyone else's. They may misinterpret the accuracy and importance of their data or a particular tool that they are using. They overestimate their skill in analyzing information. The most grandiose traders at times will even think that they are impervious to making any mistakes at all. Thoughts like these, even if they are fleeting, can result in Titanic-like disasters. Overconfidence tends to lead traders to underestimate the risks involved with trading, and that is what sets them up for failure.

Meanwhile, during my interviews with successful market traders, time and again I heard the words, "Respect the market," and, "Only the market knows." Successful traders are not overly confident, and in fact, quite surprisingly, they are very humble in recognizing their own limitations as traders. (Note how this is different from being low in vulnerability, represented by the N6 facet.)

One of the classic scenarios of over-confidence is that of "beginner's luck." As a novice trader, one does not yet have a full appreciation for how difficult and how risky trading really is. A beginner has not yet been burned big time. In this circumstance a relative newbie who—by luck and luck alone—has a string of several winning trades in a row is bound to develop a sense of overconfidence. "This isn't all that hard. I can do this!" The higher in C1 the trader is, the more likely he is to fall prey to this trap. He is more apt to attribute his early success to some special talent or insight and fail to realize the components of luck, timing, chance, and serendipity.

You can probably already guess the next step. Being overconfident in his early good fortune, such a trader quickly becomes more aggressive and takes on larger positions in subsequent trades— only to be entirely wiped out and forced to stop trading once he hits rock bottom. This same predictable pattern plays out more times than you can imagine. Even if you no longer consider yourself a rookie at this point in your trading career, there is still a lesson to be learned from this classic rookie blunder, as overconfidence will pop up even in the best and most seasoned of traders.

How big a problem is overconfidence in trading? UC Berkeley School of Business professor Terrance Odean has conducted numerous research studies on trading. In fact, he is often credited with having done more research on the behaviors and habits of individual traders than anyone else. Odean says, "Our central message is that trading is hazardous to your wealth. Specifically, a large fraction of day traders, more than eight out of ten, lose money, though a small fraction of day traders earn large and persistent profits."[2]

How to become one of the small fraction and not end up in the 80 percent bracket of losers? Odean's research suggests that overconfidence plays an important role in enticing new traders to enter into the investment arena, an arena where less than 20 percent are profitable (after costs). Some of Odean's other studies in behavioral finance find that around 74 percent of all fund managers self-rate their own trading prowess as "above average" in comparison to other fund managers. Of course that is not mathematically possible, as obviously only half of traders can statistically be better than the other half. So we can see from Odean's data that there is both a lot of overconfidence and a lot of failure going on in trading.

Overconfidence can easily lead to overtrading, although often the trait of impulsivity reinforces overtrading behaviors (as we talked about earlier, in the neuroticism chapter). A trader who believes her abilities are better than average will trade more frequently. But frequent trading also means more trading commissions (which reduces profits in the long run, usually) and an increased likelihood of an emotional blunder that triggers a panic or series of subsequent bad decisions in other trades.

Basically it comes down to degree of self-control. Those market traders who are excessively high in the C facets, and in particular C1, feel a huge need for order in and control over their lives. The most overconfident of traders, thinking that they have some sort of magical ability to control the markets and see into them better than other traders, often attempt to strategically time nearly every single market move, as opposed to picking and choosing only the most prime entry points. Studies by Odeon have shown that the most active traders (top quintile) actually have 7 percent lower annual returns in comparison to the least active of traders (bottom quintile).

Another intriguing study[3] regarding trader overconfidence has something to teach us. Market traders were shown sets of fictitious, randomly generated price patterns and asked to figure out the market's next direction and indicate their confidence in their predictions. Traders with the highest confidence in their predictions, not only traded the most frequently, but also incurred the greatest losses! Not only did they have more losing trades, but the mounting cost of trading commissions was also a major problem for the overconfident trader.

The point we are trying to make is not that you should strip away all your self-esteem and confidence in your trading abilities. Of course not. In fact, our own findings actually show that great market traders are, by and large, slightly more confident (slightly higher in C1) than the mean of the general population, based on NEO-AC findings. But they have a different kind of confidence. And it's how they apply their confidence that really matters.

The great traders we interviewed consistently talked about their confidence in being able to manage whatever comes up, whatever crisis that arises, or whatever corner they paint themselves into. Yes, they are certain in their trading abilities, but they are also confident that they can be flexible, ready to adapt and improvise when needed. That's reflected in their low N6 vulnerability scores. In a nutshell, they have confidence that they will know how to get themselves out of a jam when it occurs, and they know that that those jams are going to occur! Great traders learn to balance their high confidence with reality-based prudence and wisdom.

What can be learned from this knowledge of great traders? Those of us who are high in C1 will benefit from practicing humility while trading. If you are high in C1 and have a winning trade on, be glad, but don't get too cocky. Always keep in mind that the markets are bigger than you and at any moment may make a move you are not anticipating. No matter how many winning trades you have had this month, the markets are always capable of swallowing up your profits all at once. So be on guard. Act not in an arrogant or entitled way; show respect for the markets. Appreciate your own limitations and be psychologically nimble and ready to alter your approach to the markets when you get into a jam.

Those high in C1 should especially pay attention when you are on a roll—when you have had several winning trades in a row. That's when your overconfidence can translate into careless sloppiness. This is when you let your guard down, leave a position open longer than you meant to, and then take a big hit.

A great NFL football coach knows and appreciates the talents of his players. Internally he can be very confident in them. However, before every Sunday game he will repeatedly tell the media and his players, and even tell himself, how good the upcoming opponent is. He will purposefully minimize the talent of his own team and focus instead on how big a challenge the opposing team is. Every week he makes it sound as if this is going to be the most difficult game of the season. He will name all the players on the other team when he is especially wary of and knows will pose the biggest threats. This is what any wise coach, football or otherwise, does.

In particular if you have a combination of high C1 and high N5 (impulsivity), you really need to be sure you think before you leap. You are a trader who is especially prone to rash decisions based on overconfidence. This combination of tending to be impulsive and overconfident can spell extra big trouble. So be extra deliberate in all your ways. In fact, make a point of taking a brief pause or cooling off period before you plunge your money into that trade that feels like "a sure thing."

For example, if while staring at the charts on your computer monitor, you feel a sudden impulse to act on a "sure-thing" trade because you feel invincible and on top of the world, step back. Walk to the kitchen for a few minutes and drink a tall glass of cold ice water. Remind yourself that there will always be plenty of future opportunities that will be as good as (if not better than) this one. Tell yourself it is better to be safe than sorry. Coach yourself. Ask yourself if you have really taken the time needed to examine the trade from a logical perspective and not just an emotional one. Have you really assessed and sized up just how dangerous a trade it is and what the potential threats in the market are? Have you really stepped back to analyze whether you are being overconfident? Are you ready and able to be flexible enough to change your plans if the market suddenly turns against you? And (this is crucial, so pay attention here) if your emotional mind tries to convince your logical mind that there isn't enough time to do all of that right now, that you are going to miss the boat if you don't act now and place the trade, then clearly something is amiss. Do not make the trade.

A very helpful task in any decision-making process is to take a piece of blank paper and draw a line down the middle. Write the pros and the cons for making the decision on each side of the line, and then compare them side by side to see which side of the line has more evidence.

Either mentally or on real paper you can go through this exercise when trying to decide about placing trades, too. On the left side make a list of the actual evidence you have *for* making the trade. On the right side make a list of the evidence that argues *against* making the trade. It's OK to put both logical reasons ("I'm heading out of town tomorrow and realistically I don't think I will have time to closely follow this trade if I am in it") and emotional reasons ("This is the best trading signal I have seen all month, and regretting missing it would make me feel worse than if it turns out to be a bust") on your two lists, but be sure to recognize and designate which ones are which. By actually taking the time to make a quick list like this, you are analyzing the situation and removing two of the biggest threats to your success—overconfidence and impulsivity. Bottom line, if the left side of the paper does not strongly and clearly outweigh the right side, do not execute the trade!

This technique of making pro and con lists is another one of the cornerstones of CBT. The more your practice it, the more adept you will become at recognizing pitfalls you may not have otherwise noticed. Many of us already make such lists in our heads when trying to make decisions. However, the research shows that putting the pros and cons into tangible lists, that is, writing them down on a piece of paper in front of you, where you can actually compare them side by side and decide which list holds more weight, is far more effective than making mental lists.

Finally, aside from these lists, look yourself in the eye and ask yourself bluntly if you are really showing enough respect for the markets, or if you are just feeling cocky, and possibly even deceiving yourself. Examine your motives in the moment. Assess how honest you are being with yourself. At all times practice *awareness*. That is, be aware of all the possible trading risks. If there is any doubt, do not enter the trade. Tell yourself again: There will be plenty more good trades to come down the pike.

If you come to a point where you catch yourself repeatedly acting in an arrogant manner, take an extended time out. Exit all of your trades and cease all further trading until you develop a new-found respect for the markets.

Now, on the other hand if you are actually low in the C1 facet, be aware that you have a propensity to doubt yourself and be underconfident. You are the trader who, despite having a plethora of data telling you to take a position in the market, still finds it hard to "pull the trigger." You may question your ability to analyze the data appropriately and come to the right conclusion. You may wonder whether you are still missing or overlooking something, despite the fact you have done all your homework. To combat this trait, you need to spend time reminding yourself that you are prepared, capable, and competent (assuming that you actually are).

If you are low in C1, using the CBT methods described earlier in the book, repeat this mantra over and over: There are no sure things in trading the markets, and nobody has access to an ultimate truth that will unlock the secret to the markets, but I have been thorough and careful in my work. I am capable. I am competent.

For you low C1 traders out there, even when a trade turns out to be a lemon, take courage in the fact that at least you were well prepared for battle and that, whatever the cause of your defeat, you will learn from it and apply it to the next battle (and make lemonade). Just as a great football coach is able to instill new confidence in his discouraged team coming off a big loss, so too do you have a mental need to give yourself pep talks to remind yourself that you actually can succeed in trading the markets. This is especially true after a losing trade, as this is when you may be prone to doubting your abilities to study the markets and identify a winner to get you back on track. You must not allow this self-doubt trait to prevent you from taking the next good trade.

Another possible tactic for the underconfident trader is to join a trading group, take on a mentor, or even enlist the services of a friend, spouse, or other loved one who can provide you with some positive feedback and remind you that you actually do have desirable trading skills. Put yourself in a position where you can demonstrate to others (people whom you admire) that you have sharp trading skills. As they report this back to you, this will only build up your confidence.

Mental Edge Tips
- Match your trading style to your personality. Highly conscientious individuals make better systems traders, while those low in C make better discretionary traders. If you are somewhere in the middle on C, be sure you are blending the two styles.
- The tendency to be overly confident has been shown by many researchers to be a huge problem for many traders and portends losses in the markets. While anyone has the potential to be overly confident from time to time, some of us have personalities that are prone to this. C1 is the facet that will compare you to others.
- While the great traders tend to have slightly higher than average C1 scores, they consistently demonstrate an ability to integrate this trait into healthy and adaptive ways of approaching the markets with great respect. You should, too.
- Show respect for the markets. But also have confidence that you have the skills and brainpower to get yourself out of a jam when it does arise.
- Win or lose, you are your own coach. Whenever you are contemplating a move in the markets, clearly look at both the pros and cons of making it. Weigh the risks. Identify both the logical and emotional pulls that are involved in the process. By doing so, you will at least partly remove the risk of making a move based mostly on overconfidence.

CHAPTER 18

Optimism and Trading

The human trait of optimism is somewhat related to confidence but is not quite the same thing. Optimism relates more to how positive one feels about the outside world, while confidence is how positive you feel about yourself. Optimism is best accounted for on the E6 (positive emotions) facet of the NEO-AC.

People who are overly positive, or overly optimistic, tend to see the world through "rose-colored lenses." They tend to overlook, filter out, or even flat out ignore negative information, all the while seeking out evidence that confirms their positive outlook. They see what they want to see.

Traders who are high in E6 may forget about certain losing trades (or the negative consequences, punishments, or lessons related to those trades) and retain strong (maybe even exaggerated or false) memories about their winning trades. Their minds filter out data, so they see the pros and not the cons of a situation or idea. The search for confirming data and the forgetting of unsupporting data are actually a form of a psychological defense.

The human mind can be very selective about the data it takes in. An experiment at Harvard in 1999 proves the point. If you do a web search for "The Invisible Gorilla," you can learn more about, and even see with your own eyes, this experiment. In a nutshell, experiment subjects were instructed to watch a short video of a group of young people passing basketballs back and forth to each other. Half of the people in the video were dressed in white shirts; the other half were in black shirts.

Two groups of viewers watched the video. The task of one group of viewers was to count how many times the people in white shirts passed the basketball. The task of a second group of viewers was to just casually watch the video. Smack dab in the middle of the video a person dressed up in a gorilla suit and mask in plain sight walks and dances across the video screen. At one point the gorilla clearly turns and looks straight at the camera, and hence the viewers. There is no subtlety to the gorilla; he is right there staring directly at you! But it turns out that, while everyone who was asked to watch the video passively noticed the gorilla's presence, only 56 percent of the viewers who were counting ball passes noticed it. The study shows how the human brain really does filter out data and sensory input all the time—and not just minor details!

For those traders who score very high in E6 (optimism, that is, feeling overly positive and sure about the expected outcome of an event) or are very high in C1 (you have great attention to detail, but are also prone to overconfidence), there is an incredibly big chance you are going to miss the elephant (or gorilla) in the room. The overly optimistic person, it turns out, has difficulty seeing or accepting something that may be plainly obvious to others.

Keep in mind that it's not that the person is blind to the evidence or not smart enough to understand it. The gorilla is right in front of him, staring right at him. Rather, it's usually the result of a *need* to believe something different—to perceive a different reality or an expected course of events and outcome. Once this "need" becomes incorporated into part of his analysis, his ego gets caught up in it. As traders say, they become "married to their opinions." They have a tough time breaking away from their preconceived notions.

Some of us are more prone than others to trading the markets with this kind of bias, based on personality traits. It's very easy for some of us to become entirely focused on and convinced of an idea in the markets (either bullish or bearish), especially if we have a built-in set of behaviors and beliefs that continually filter out the same sort of input over and over. We will tend to look for the same chart patterns or indicator readings, when really a good trader is always trying to broaden his horizon and see the markets from multiple as well as fresh perspectives.

The best traders, from our interviews with them, are able to recognize that they have a whole set of different brain filters. They learn to take one filter off and put another one on at their own will. This enables them to see and manipulate a wide variety of information garnered from different views of the market. You can also see how easy it is to fall into the same market traps and repeat the same mistakes over and over if you do not recognize how brains can sometimes filter information.

Here's a simple example of using different brain filters. When evaluating a potential trade, you might need to apply two different timing templates: a longer time frame template for overall market direction analysis and a shorter time frame template to time trade entry or exit. A naive trader who looks at both charts simultaneously, both the long and short frame templates, could easily get confused. If what appears to be a prime buy opportunity on a monthly or yearly chart shows up as a clear sell signal on an intraday chart, the trader could, at the very least, freeze up and miss the move or potentially even make the wrong call and buy based on the daily chart. The key is to synchronize the two time frames and take both perspectives into account at the same time. If the weekly or monthly chart is screaming "buy," but the daily chart is hollering "sell," wait until the daily chart is giving you a clear entry into the market.

Trading the markets is *nothing at all* like counting ball passes in the gorilla video in one very important way. It is easy to intently focus your attention on the basketball, ignoring the rest of the images that occur on the screen, and accurately count the number of passes. But trading the markets requires focused attention on a vast amount of information, data, and trends—all simultaneously, of course. In trading you need to be aware of virtually all movements on your screen, as well as plenty more that are not on your screen. The amount of data that your mind has to process before executing a winning trade is no trivial thing.

Again, learn to train your mind to use different "filters"—one at a time. Then learn how to amalgamate the multiple streams of data into one cohesive model or plan. Obviously, this is much easier said than done. But this is what the giants in the world of trading do. This ability to examine the markets from different angles, using and applying multiple different filters—along with sheer determination—is truly what separates great traders from the rest of the pack. None of the successful traders we interviewed said that this comes easily or naturally to them. They all confirmed that it takes a tremendous amount of focus and dedication.

Optimism, as a trait, often attracts people to jobs in business and politics. These are people who have very positive attitudes. They believe things are either going well or are going to get better. This optimism can certainly attract others to their causes. Not many politicians or CEOs are going to attract a following by preaching doom and gloom! However, when it comes to trading the markets, which is a very analytical endeavor, overly optimistic people have a tendency to rely on a sort of superficial analysis. They may deny important negative evidence going on in the markets. If your E6 score is high, watch out for this! As an overly optimistic trader, you may not be aware of growing dangers in the markets, and you may not realize just how risky or precarious your current position is. You may find yourself overexposed.

If you are high in E6, be sure that you fully evaluate both the pros and cons to any trade, trading system, or trading idea. One helpful method was described in the previous chapter, on conscientiousness. That is, whenever confronted with a potential trade or new trading idea, make a list of the evidence for it and another list of the evidence against it. Force yourself to adequately weigh the pros and cons. Those high in E6 have a tendency to overlook or ignore the cons, so force yourself to pay attention to them.

Another helpful method for those who are high in E6 (actually, it's a helpful tool for all traders, but is essential for those high in E6) is to rehearse different "what if" scenarios. For example, as you are eagerly anticipating a move in the market that you think is sure to happen, mentally rehearse and ask yourself various "what if" questions. "What if the opening price takes out yesterday's low?" "What if I don't get my order filled at price X?" By asking yourself such "what-if" scenarios (as many as you can think of), you will develop a healthy behavioral pattern of proactively preventing yourself from getting tied to fixed ideas and getting caught up in false assumptions.

If in conjunction with high E6 you are also high in the O5 facet (ideas), you are someone who may easily get swept into (and perhaps swept away by) passing fads and hype. If this is you, pay attention not to fall prey to a story or a sales pitch that is "too good to be true." For instance, don't plunk your money down for some biotech company's penny stock just because it has a business idea that sounds super unique and timely. If the company is not financially and structurally sound, this is a very risky investment, and you may not easily see it that way looking through those rose-colored lenses (E6) you have on, in addition to your openness to new ideas (O5).

On the other hand, those market traders who score low in E6 have the potential makeup to be rather pessimistic about external circumstances and events. To them, things are perpetually seen through "gray-colored lenses." The tendency here is to remain excessively grim and negativistic when a situation really does not call for it. This especially comes into play when things are starting to pick up. We all can easily identify an absolute disaster when it's right in front of us. But those traders who are low in E6 are at risk of missing out on clues that there is now a reversal in the works, that the gray clouds are starting to part and the sun is coming out. They may not realize until it is too late that the market forces are now working in their favor.

If you are low in E6, be sure to maintain an objective and non-judgmental awareness of your tendency to see things as being grim. That is, remind yourself that you tend to see the glass as being half empty. Realize that, as such, you may miss out on great trading opportunities due to your tendency to pay extra attention to negative details and attributes. One of the most effective things you can do as a pessimist is to keep a journal of your negative perceptions and relate them to how things really pan out. You may start to see patterns to how you misjudged things as being worse than they actually were. By monitoring and getting to know this trend, you can start to correct yourself in advance.

Besides seeing thing through either a rose- or a gray-colored lens, another pitfall common in one particular group of traders is seeing things through too small or narrow a lens. People who are low in O5, ideas, by definition have a tendency to be closed-minded or at least narrow-minded when it comes to thinking about things in new or different ways. We are all subject to what psychologists call "narrow framing," which is when one considers specific decisions in remote isolation without giving much regard to the bigger picture.

Investors or traders low in O5 are at particular risk of focusing in on trading decisions one at a time, without giving adequate consideration to the grander scheme of things. They may fail to see how a particular trade or investment fits into their overall trading portfolio, agrees with their particular trading philosophy, or what have you. They may even miss out on diversification opportunities with their investments because they are so closed-minded about what they are doing. For example, a long-term trader may refuse to consider short- to medium-term trading because he sees it as "too risky," when, in fact, his mind was never open enough to even consider the advantages to adding some short-term trades to his portfolio.

Mental Edge Tips
- Keep in mind, as with all personality traits, there can be both strengths and weaknesses to being either high or low in optimism. It is not necessarily more advantageous to be more optimistic or pessimistic. The key is to know yourself and learn how to apply your strengths and minimize your weaknesses.
- Learn to adopt a whole set of mental filters when analyzing market information. Try to learn new ways of seeing and interpreting things. Don't get set in your same old ways. One great way to do this is to read and incorporate the ideas and strategies of others.
- Although it's helpful to be continuously drawing from the work and ideas of other traders, ultimately, to become consistently successful, you will need to find your own unique set of mental lenses to look at the markets through. (Growing up, I can't tell you how many of my father's students hoped to emulate him. But his best students—those who really made careers out of trading the markets—were the ones who incorporated my dad's ideas, and others', into their own. Nobody will ever be very successful trying to mimic a Michael Jordan.)

CHAPTER 19

Excitement-Seeking and Trading

It is rather unlikely that you, as a market speculator, score low in the E5 facet (excitement-seeking). More than likely your E5 score is either average or high.

As mentioned earlier, E5 is the facet that portrays a person's tendency to seek out thrills and rushes. It also heavily influences the likelihood of someone developing a problem with or even an addiction to trading—that is, turning the art and science of market trading it into something more akin to gambling.

For traders with an E5 score on the high side, there's a sneaky mental trap you need to be mindful of. You may find yourself placing trades, not because the market is ripe for a trade, but because you are attempting to fulfill emotional gratification that is not being met in the rest of your life.

For example, if you are stuck in a marriage or other relationship that has lost its sizzle, you may turn to the markets to fill that void of excitement. And certainly trading can provide the excitement you are longing for. Even if you are not flat-out addicted to the markets and even if you are not trading solely as a way to make yourself feel better, if you are high in E5, you may turn to the markets as a readily accessible venue to find some quick stimulation of the reward center of the brain, a.k.a. the amygdala. Be careful that you are not seeking excitement by placing trades that really should not be placed. Watch out for this!

One simple way to combat this trap is to make sure that you turn to other sources of excitement in your life. Trading should be your job, not your drug. If your life or marriage needs more excitement infused into it, be sure you are either addressing it directly, or at the very least, finding alternative yet more healthy avenues to seek out exciting times. Don't turn to the markets for this, as it is a sure recipe for financial disaster. You've heard of "cheap thrills." For many—especially those high in E5—the markets all too easily become a source of "expensive thrills."

Keep in mind, too, that our survey of great market traders shows that they score average in the E5 domain of personality. Hence, compared to gamblers who score high in E5, they are less prone to trading the markets as a compensatory mechanism for lack of excitement in other areas of their lives. They have less of a need to seek out excitement.

Furthermore, the research out there shows that excitement-seeking is also a huge risk factor for overtrading, as is the case with overconfidence. So for anyone who is especially high in both E5 and C1, this is really something to watch out for. An example where this comes up is when the excitement-seeker places trades that don't follow or conform to his system, all because the system is not producing enough trades on its own to satisfy the active, invigorating trading style this kind of trader wants and needs. Or he may over trade during periods when the market is less volatile in an attempt to "liven things up." So if you are high in conscientiousness (C) and excitement-seeking (E5), be sure to choose a system that trades frequently enough to satisfy your brain's need for excitement.

Mental Edge Tips
- Don't use the markets as your recreational playground or vehicle for pleasure or excitement-seeking. View your trading life as your job, and not a pastime.
- If you find that you are turning to the markets to seek out thrills, one of the best things you can do is seek out relatively safer ways to experience those kinds of sensations. Go visit your local skydiving school, if that's what it takes. Seriously! By finding other ways to fill voids in your life, you are less prone to using the markets as a drug.
- If you are high in excitement-seeking (E5), recognize the risks, but also be sure to adopt a trading style or system that will keep up with your "need for speed."

CHAPTER 20

The Secret to Happiness

What is the secret to happiness in this world? Lots of people will be more than happy to sell you their purported secrets to enduring happiness. But you are about to find out what the scientific research says about the matter.

Subjective life satisfaction (SLS) is the researcher's measure of well-being and is used commonly in what is known as "happiness economics." It is also sometimes referred to as subjective well-being. There are formal scales that measure it.

SLS in essence represents how satisfied a person feels with life generally, as contrasted with *positive affect* (PA), which represents how happy a person feels at any single point in time. Overall life satisfaction involves people thinking about their lives as a whole, taking into account such factors such as whether they are achieving their personal goals, whether they are doing as well as other people around them, and whether they are happy generally, rather than just right now. Life satisfaction is thus a longer-term measure than affect.

The "big two" personality domains, neuroticism (N) and extroversion (E), relate to both SLS and PA. A study done by Costa and McRea[1] (inventors of the NEO-AC) back in 1980 showed that both N and E scores are able to predict differences in happiness or life satisfaction and unhappiness or life dissatisfaction in people 10 years in advance! Yep, researchers can actually tell by personality testing who is going to be more satisfied with life and who is not.

But the science of happiness goes beyond that. There is a growing body of evidence that suggests that the three key components to
long-term happiness (SLS) in life include:

1. The ability to pursue autonomous goals
2. A sense of mastery or skill in something that is meaningful
3. The experience of feelings of relatedness with other people

First off, it is interesting that making money is *not* one of the
key ingredients to long-term happiness. Second, it should be noted
that autonomy and mastery are two features that can be very compatible with market trading. The markets offer a great place to find
and develop these.

Autonomy means that you are responsible for your own
actions and decisions. The markets provide just such a venue. When
it comes down to placing a trade, it is you and only you who can
pull the trigger. You may have gathered information and advice
from various sources, but in the end it is you who will make the
decision. And it is you who will have to live with that decision, for
better or worse. As a full-time trader, you are your own boss. You
show up to work at the hours you want and the hours you think
are going to be most productive. Thanks to modern technology,
you can trade from the quiet and comfort of your own house, or
you can trade from within the walls of a crowded and noisy coffee
shop. You take trading vacations when you want to, not when the
boss man tells you to.

Most important of all, as a professional trader, your job allows
you to engage in trading the markets the way you want to and not
the way you are told to by a superior. As a trader, you are running
a one-person enterprise where you make all the calls. In fact, there
is more autonomy working as a trader than just about any business
startup you can imagine. Why? Because as a trader you have no
customers to satisfy. No employees to manage. No overhead. No
warehouse. Plus there's minimal bookkeeping and minimal need
for specialized equipment or technology. Trading is the ultimate
private enterprise for the individual who truly likes to operate on
her own.

As for mastery of a skill, there is no doubt that every human
being has a built-in drive to do something well. When I was a child,

my father told me over and over, "I don't care what you do with your life, as long as you do it very well. Even if you are a ditch digger, as long as you're the best ditch digger you can be, you will be happy." How wise my father's words were, and they are the same words I instill in my own children and indeed in many of my patients as well.

One of the key secrets to finding happiness in this world truly is in creating your own sense of identity, and the way you do that is by being a master at whatever it is you do. By becoming a master at something, you will have found success; you will define yourself as being successful. And this will make you happy. It doesn't matter what it is: For some it may be mastering the art of home-making, or restoring old hotrods, or learning a new language. For others that mastery may be in learning the most about the markets. Because the markets offer such a giant intellectual and psychological challenge, the happiness rewards reaped from learning about and understanding them can also be quite immense.

Often times people feel disappointed that they are not making as much money in the markets as they would like to or had anticipated making. But they fail to take into account that the vast majority of people who try to take on the markets end up failing miserably and losing money. So merely breaking even trading the markets, in a very real sense, indicates a certain level of mastery and competence. And yet nobody trades the markets to break even. So there's a bit of a disconnect here. On a psychological level, once you can get beyond the making money component of trading and focus more on the mastery part of it, you will be a happier trader, no matter what your trading portfolio is doing. And in the long run, happier traders make for more prudent, careful, and successful traders.

The third component to long-term happiness, feelings of relatedness to others, is something that is going to be more difficult for many personal traders to experience. Usually they have to go out and seek it. If you feel you have an autonomous life from trading and are a master of the markets but are still not happy in your life, look here to this third piece of the happiness puzzle. Find ways to interact with others, regardless of whether this means socializing with others about the markets or simply getting involved with a volunteering project, going to a church or synagogue, or what have you.

For those who are lower in N and higher in E, SLS (happiness) is going to come easier to you. For the rest of us, we need to work on it a bit! Trading may not always be profitable (obviously), but it is crucial that your involvement in the markets contribute to your overall sense of autonomy and competence. We can hope that trading will also provide you experiences of personal relatedness and fulfillment, as well.

The act of trading simply as a way to make money likely will be an unfulfilling endeavor and not provide you with long-term happiness. If, as a trader, you find yourself struggling to be able to continuously dip your cup into the three wells of happiness (autonomy, mastery, and relatedness), this line of work may not be for you. If you consistently are experiencing negative emotions while trading (regardless of the outcomes of the trades themselves), you may want to ask yourself whether this is the right path or if some other pursuit may be more appropriate for you. Life should be fun. Trading should be fun. If you are not sensing fun in your career as a trader, a careful reassessment and reallocation of your resources may be needed.

A helpful technique to better assess and track your emotional responses to trading is to keep a daily journal or log of your feelings. There are fancy (and expensive) computer software programs on the market that you can invest in, but really all you need is a notebook and pencil. The best way to go about doing this is to track your emotions before, during, and at the end of your trading day. It doesn't have to be excessively detailed, and you don't have to worry about grammar; this is not going to be read or used by anyone but you. You can even develop your own scales for rating the different moods you have during your trading day. Also, make sure you take notes as to how your trading performance was each day and correlate it to your fluctuations in mood. Keep such a journal for at least a month, if not longer.

Some sample questions that you will want to ask yourself every time you make a journal entry include:

1. Did I feel either happy or sad while trading today? What was it that made me feel that way?
2. Did I feel anxious or stressed out while trading today? What triggered that?

3. Did I feel alert and energetic when trading today? Did I do anything different today?

4. Did I feel discouraged while I was trading today? How did I overcome it?

5. Did I feel capable of succeeding at my trading today?

6. Did I blame myself today when my trading didn't work out as planned? Was I really to blame?

7. Did I feel satisfied with my trading results today? Did I meet my goals? Did I even have any set goals for today?

8. Did I feel angry, edgy, or frustrated when trading today? Who or what was I angry at? How did I deal with those emotions? Was it healthy how I dealt with my emotions?

9. Did I feel in control of what happened in my trading today? Was it sustained?

10. Did I make impulsive decisions while I was trading today? How could I have prevented that?

Once you have tallied your emotional responses for some period of time, you will get a better sense of whether your negative moods and emotions (anxiety, anger, hostility, doubt, guilt) emerge primarily in the context of losing trades, or if you experience such negative emotions no matter what your market performance is.

If, overall, you tend to have positive feelings while trading (no matter whether you are losing money or not and no matter whether it is still a lot of "hard work"), you can assure yourself that you are engaged in a healthy and appropriate activity. In this positive state of mind, you will be more potent and effective as a trader.

Mihaly Csikszentmihalyi, a Hungarian psychologist who has studied and written extensively on happiness and creativity, has shown that performance (and this applies to athletes, artists, chess players, managers, and anyone else) is optimized when one is experiencing himself positively.

If, however, you have a preponderance of negative feelings while trading the markets (again, especially if it is regardless of the outcomes of your trades), you need to appreciate that trading is detracting from your overall well-being as a person. Your performance will also be hindered, as your negative emotions are likely going to interfere with your cognitive abilities to master the markets (concentration, pattern recognition, judgment, planning, and calculations), and you will likely not be a successful trader. In the end, your negative emotions are going to get the best of you and your trades.

Finally, keep in mind that emotions are fundamental in investing and trading. Emotions such as greed, regret, fear, anger, panic, surprise, excitement, relief, and skepticism are all natural emotions that all traders have from time to time. Although these emotions can certainly sabotage the best-laid trading plans, these emotions can also be invaluable in helping you understand yourself and your trading habits better. Learn to accept these emotions (*all* of them), because they will help you learn faster about yourself, what style of trading best works for you, how you make the same mistakes over and over, and so forth. Do not shun the emotional part of trading. Recording emotions in a log or journal may seem "sissy," but actually it is one of the best ways that you can learn to deal with your emotions instead of reacting to them.

Mental Edge Tips
- Your ability to be happy doing what you are doing is going to have a huge effect on your ability to do it.
- Make sure that you are having fun and enjoy being a trader, regardless of your actual performance.
- To become a happier trader (which, in the end, will parlay into you becoming a more successful trader), always strive to include a healthy and balanced portion of autonomy, mastery, and relatedness in your daily life.
- This is not rocket science here, but all too often traders are so caught up in striking it rich via trading the markets or developing the latest, greatest trading system that they totally neglect commonsense advice. Anyone who is not happy in his or her current job, regardless of the salary, should be thinking of making either a job change or a career change. The same goes for the job of trading the markets.

CHAPTER 21

The Overly Dependent Trader

There is a constellation of personality traits that places a person at risk of becoming excessively dependent on others.

First let's define the differences between dependent and independent traders. The dependent trader is always looking for quick, easy, and instant profits, without putting in the legwork to earn them. He follows the crowd, especially the crowd that is wrong. He gets into trades based not on real knowledge or wisdom, but on the latest "hot tip" or what he perceives as "insider information" which in fact is nothing more than worthless information that everyone has access to. The dependent trader often turns to fully automated (no effort or thinking required) and overhyped trading systems that promise the moon. Dependent traders trade without their own plans and with little or no understanding of what they are doing. They constantly listen to the advice of various financial pundits and news broadcasters airing "expert" views. As such, they easily get sucked into following the masses into dead-end trades or even ruin.

Independent traders are industrious; they work hard and enthusiastically for everything they desire and get. Independent traders still have some dependence (we all do), but they more appropriately know how and when to seek help and learn from other traders. They will go out of their way to seek people who can educate them in how to be a better trader, not which trades to place. Independent traders are willing to take risks in their efforts and work hard, as they clearly know that often we learn more from failures and mistakes than we do from successes. At the same time, they try their best not to repeat the same mistakes over and over.

What NEO-AC facets are involved with dependency? Traders who measure high in N facets (negative emotions and especially the N1 facet of anxiety) are high in E1 (warmth), low in E3 (assertiveness), and high in A facets (especially A1, trust), are especially vulnerable to this kind of detrimental behavior.

Let's discuss the concept of mentorship. Dependent traders are those who have a need to be constantly reassured by others, and in particular by those whom they look up to (mentors, teachers, or even "gurus"). Now, there is nothing wrong with having a mentor, as long as the mentorship relationship is a healthy one—where there are clear definitions of the role of each party.

Overly dependent traders, conversely, enter into such a relationship mostly because of a need for frequent reassurance that they are doing the right thing. They may, in fact, possess a very reasonable trading plan of their own. They may even have a very specific potential trade in mind. But they experience too much anxiety over asserting themselves in the markets if they don't first get a "stamp of approval" from someone else—someone who serves as a sort of authority figure.

Prior to placing a trade, overly dependent traders feel compelled to "run it by" other traders to see what they think of it or what they would do. But by asking for input from others, dependent traders can start to lose focus on their own understanding of the market. They can become confused, or even overwhelmed, by varying opinions and different perspectives on a particular market scenario. They can lose touch with their own trading plan.

Such investors tend to spend far too much time reading self-help trading books, trying to get access to well-known traders from whom they hope to "squeeze" as much information and insight as they can, and so on. By doing such they never truly develop their own unique trading styles that work for them—all because they are too busy trying to emulate or adapt someone else's style.

If you are anywhere within this camp of developing dependency on other traders, be aware of the potential pitfalls. If you do feel you need mentorship (and you may), make sure you keep to the following principals:

1. Find a mentor that works for you. A good mentor is never a crutch. A good mentor is someone who inspires you and entices you to learn more, blaze your own path, and develop your own style of trading.

2. Limit the number of mentors you have. That's not to say that you must totally isolate yourself from different ideas (you don't have to cancel your various subscriptions to trading magazines and burn the numerous trading courses you may have already bought). But for true mentorship, keep it clean and simple. Rely on just a few true mentors to inspire you.

3. The best trading mentors will actually teach you how to develop "self-mentorship." That is, healthy mentorship is not indefinite and never-ending. Your mentor should be teaching you how to take on the role of being your own coach.

   Think of this as learning how to fly an airplane. You certainly want to have your coach behind the controls the very first time you go up in the air. You probably want your coach to give you the controls the second time, but eventually you hope your coach will teach you how to fly all by yourself, and you will go on to be a coach or mentor for someone else. So once you are able to fly confidently by yourself, cut your ties with your mentor. You don't want your flight instructor in the cockpit with you forever, as this will only prove to be annoying (at best) or unhealthy (at worst).

4. Once you earn your wings, become a mentor to someone else. This will help you continue to grow in your understanding of the markets (and simultaneously increase your own subjective life satisfaction!).

5. Do not depend upon only one method or style of trading. Learn different trading techniques and compare them.

Your chances for success as a trader greatly increase if you have decent insight into multiple trading methodologies and styles, especially when using fundamental or technical indicators. It's good to have some fundamental knowledge of all types of trading before you specialize and adopt the style that works best for you.

Mental Edge Tips
- Recognize when mentorship has gone awry. If you are not sure, ask your mentor. Ask him if he feels you are too reliant on him, annoying to him, or not growing in your own right.
- The best way to continue learning something is to become a teacher of it, and the best way to test your knowledge or fluency of any subject is to try and explain it to someone else. Becoming a trading mentor to someone else will pay dividends.

CHAPTER 22

A Case Study: Larry Williams

We all learn best by using examples and looking at models. And what better way to learn how personality influences trading style and success than to carefully dissect the personality of one of the world's greatest living traders? Luckily I have at my disposal my father, Larry Williams.

In order to better understand how a serious and experienced trader can make use of personality testing, Pops agreed to go under the "personality microscope" known as the NEO-AC, as well to engage in a discussion about what his results mean to him and how he has seen his personality traits at work as a market trader. I think you will benefit from observing how this process works.

First some background. As many of you may know, my father is quite well regarded as an individual futures market trader. That is, he primarily trades his own money for himself. He has been doing it for a long time, in fact well before I was born. He (still) holds the record for best performance ever in the Robbins World Trading Cup, when in 1987 he turned $10,000 into over $1 million in just one year. He is also known for his "Million Dollar Challenges"—in which, to prove he is a genuine market trader and not some guy who makes all his money selling books and lecturing, he bravely trades a million dollars' worth of real futures contracts live, in front of his students—and he lets them keep 20 percent of the profits!

To be clear, Dad is much more than a market trader. He has had his hands in so many different projects and endeavors over the years, from politics to boxing promoter to far flung Indiana Jones-like treasure hunting expeditions, that it's impossible to try to define Dad. He is a unique, one of a kind marvel. But at the end of the day, the one activity that Dad keeps coming back to, the one hat that he can never put down, is being a futures trader. It's what he enjoys the most and what he is best at.

Of course my father, like all traders, has had his share of losing trades, market heartbreaks, large drawdowns, and mindless blunders. If you have ready any of his books, you know he does not hide his mistakes from his students. But you would be hard-pressed to find a genuine market speculator who has been more consistently successful over as long a period of time as my father has been, this being his sixth decade as a full-time trader. Growing up as his son, watching Dad go through such dramatic ups and downs in his life, often I was left scratching my head as to the motivations and meanings of some of his behaviors, ideas, and emotions. As I became educated and trained as a psychiatrist, I began to learn more about what makes my very unique dad "tick" and how my position as a psychiatrist can actually assist him in having a better understanding of himself.

Even then, it was only *after* he took the full NEO-AC that aspects of his personality were laid open and really elucidated. The NEO-AC helped explained how and why he trades the markets, what makes him a winning trader, what things he needs to avoid, and what he still needs to work on to hone his craft as a trader. His personality test results were illuminating, not only to me, but more important, they explained a lot to him. He was stunned by the insight that the personality test afforded him, and he asked that I share his results with you in order that you, too, might gain a deeper appreciation of personality.

To be sure, the goal of this chapter is *not* for you to learn to trade like Larry. Nor is it for you to try to take on exactly the same personality as Larry. There is only one Larry, and besides, you are largely stuck with the personality you were given. The purpose here is to help you understand how to interpret and then apply the results of professional personality testing to trading the markets. My father did not take his NEO-AC until 2010. I can only wonder how much more successful a trader he would have been if he had these insights going back to the 1960s, when he first set out to tame the markets! My father's comments and insights are provided for your further understanding as well.

NEUROTICISM

My father's overall neuroticism score is only moderately low ($N = 54$). This means that, in general, he does not experience strong negative emotions in response to stressful situations. The breakdown of Dad's N score by facets is interesting. He is low in anxiety ($N1 = 6$), anger ($N2 = 7$), and depression ($N3 = 4$), and very low in vulnerability ($N6 = 3$). These are critical human emotions that often get in the way of the cognitive processes (higher cortical functions) of trading. For reference, keep in mind that $N1$ and $N6$ were the two neuroticism facet scores that were low or very low across the board for our successful traders.

When a trade turns bad, negative feelings—anxiety, depression, and anger—can really cause a snowball effect, as one is no longer able to cognitively function at full capacity. In Dad's case, this is something he does not have to work on so much; he has an innate ability to keep those feelings in check during stressful times.

But of all the neuroticism facets it is in the domain of vulnerability ($N6 = 3$) that he scores the lowest. This is a very low vulnerability score. And remember, it's the extreme scores that are most telling. People who score very low in vulnerability, like Dad, perceive themselves as being capable of handling themselves in difficult situations. They feel invulnerable. Don't confuse this with a person's level of confidence, which is measured on the conscientiousness (C) scale. A very low $N6$ means that my father does not feel weak when confronted by challenging, or even emergently precarious, situations. In fact, he thrives and probably prides himself on being able to handle such stressful times. However, too much of anything is not good. If he is not careful, this trait can also work against him. A very low $N6$ can indicate that a person is at risk of failing to appreciate his own limitations. On an emotional level there may be times when he does not recognize the signs of a failing or losing trade.

LARRY: Until now I did not see the downside, that if I think I am capable of handling a difficult situation, then I tend to not pass them by. My adventures in Turkey, Iran, and Saudi Arabia (see *The Gold of Exodus* by Howard Blum), along with my treasure-hunting expeditions in the southwestern United States are great examples of me not perceiving danger and feeling invulnerable. Similarly, my two failed runs for the United States Senate in my home state of Montana, while an amazing experience, were ill fated. Like Don Quixote, I now see these very low readings probably overrode whatever intelligence I should have applied to the facts at hand.

It is one thing to do things that make others shake their heads at my actions. But only all too often, as in my IRS battle, I was shaking my own head at the things I did. But it also has a good side; nobody with my simple background would be expected to ever do the things I have done in life (become a trader, author, and so on), so the the feeling of being impervious that governs my emotions does have a healthy side. I now see—I hope—how to use this force more positively.

Fortunately for my father, in trading there is the concept of a "stop loss." He has learned to use this simple trading mechanism on any and all trades he places. It's a very handy safety brake that is automatically engaged when a trade starts failing and his emotions (especially his low scores on the N facets) don't pick up on it in time, such as when he is feeling invulnerable. In fact, if you read my father's books, you will learn that the art of money management and limiting losses by utilizing stops is a *very* important component of his trading style—just as important, if not more, as the buy and sell patterns he uses.

LARRY: My early lack of intelligence as a trader resulted in some massive profits—and massive losses—as I did not use stop losses or intelligent risk control. It was not my intelligence that eventually won the day; it was my drive to survive and learn how to bypass all the wild emotions that markets swings can cause. Being burned is how I learned. I studied my winning campaigns, but was more diligent in analyzing my losses.

My father actually scores high on one of the neuroticism facets. That is on impulsivity (N5 = 19). High impulsivity scorers tend to have difficulty controlling their urges to do something. They leap before they look. This one-two combo of high impulsivity and low vulnerability could potentially be quite problematic. Although his N5 score is not extreme, it is high enough that it could get someone into hot water from time to time. In trading, this would pan out as entering (or exiting) a trade without first fully evaluating the situation, and it often results in overtrading. The impulsive trader has to make the extra effort to restrain his urges.

> LARRY: This was even more so when I was younger. Getting beat up by the markets may be one of the best ways to adapt to your personality, better than anything my son ever studied at the ivory towers of Johns Hopkins. I eventually learned, as all successful traders do, that there are rules to winning as a trader and that some strategies just don't work. I feel that the markets have definitely altered my personality, and I was lucky that I was making money early on, because I have seen some people destroyed by early failure in the markets. In trading, even now, I have the urge to plunge. I guess it is stronger in me than in most people, which means I need to learn more control of it than most people do.

Again, it is possible for one's higher cortical functions (intelligence) to override one's feelings. This takes training, experience, and, probably more important, it takes great insight. The impulsive person has to first realize and admit to himself that he is prone to making rash decisions—such as plunging recklessly into trades that he has no business getting into. Second, he needs to identify what it is that is prompting him to impulsively place a trade. Can he identify a trigger or scenario that repeatedly causes him to leap? Last, he needs to install some kind of monitoring system that will "ring a bell" the next time such a situation arises. And it is only through this process that a highly impulsive trader matures, growing in his understanding of his innate traits and how to use them to his advantage. Remember that impulsivity, to the right degree and applied correctly and with wisdom, can also be extremely advantageous to trading the markets. It's harnessing it and applying it at the right time that matters.

> LARRY: I have certainly set up my own set of warning "bells"—I even repeat certain key phrases that are triggered when this part of my personality tries to kick me out of the driver's seat. While I always use stops, in the past I had a tendency to move them (back them off) as the market approached them. Sure, that was helpful:

about two out of every hundred times. Now when I "see" myself doing that, I repeat my promise, "never again, Larry, you know this is a sucker's play."

EXTRAVERSION

My father scores very high on the total extraversion scale (E = 147). In fact, he scored the maximum points possible on both the warmth (E1) and positive emotions (E6) scales. Anytime someone maxes out on a facet, you want to pay particular attention, as very few people max out on a facet. So something is going on here. Of these two maxed-out scores, E6 probably comes into play the most in trading the markets.

Being that high in positive emotions, my father has a tendency to feel overly happy, cheerful, and optimistic. You may be asking yourself, "Is it even possible to be too happy and cheerful in life?" Wouldn't it be a good thing to score a whopping 32 on the positive emotions scale? Wouldn't we all want that?

But remember, a person with an E6 score of 32 is frequently going to be viewing his world through rose-colored lenses. He is at risk of overlooking or filtering out the negative aspects of situations. Having an extremely high E6 score, in conjunction with low N scores, and in particular the low vulnerability score, suggests that Dad may neglect bad, dangerous, or harmful things. Even when he does see dangers for what they are, he may underestimate their ability to have a negative effect on him, as he may feel impervious to them.

> LARRY: Reading this is painful, to have a son I love be able to see right through to the center of all my faults. He is correct. I think I handle my extraversion better now than I did in my youth. And I also think that, had I realized this trait in my youth, I never would have become a "public figure" commodity guy. At times I wish I had chosen to take the more profitable route of being a money manager. But I also realize that would have been very difficult, unless I would have worked through these personality aspects. For a while I did manage funds, but soon learned it was not for me. Why this was so was a mystery. And what I could have done to alter that escaped me, until just now, seeing my personality scores. In short, I was unable to clearly see my weaknesses,

so it was nearly impossible to respond in a more correct fashion. It turns out I have allowed my positive expectations to override good judgment. Yet, a trader needs to be positive, not necessarily about the current trade, but about the fact he or she will be successful and become a winning trader.

Again, in conjunction with a very low N6 (vulnerability) score, his very high E6 underscores the importance of my father placing stop losses with his trades; he will be the first to tell you how *huge* this is. Stops are an incredibly important tool that will limit the hits he may take during times he is feeling invulnerable to stress (very low N6) or because he is thinking everything is going along fine with his trade (very high E6). Stop losses are a defense strategy that he has learned to master, as they help him limit the influence of his temperament on his trading. Over the decades of learning how to expertly apply stop losses, my father probably never even realized he was very low in N6 and very high in E6. It was only after taking the NEO-AC that it crystallized in his mind why stops are so critical for his personal temperament and trading style.

> LARRY: Point well taken. Definitely I have learned that I cannot count on my positive attitude to ensure market profits, and this is one more reason I need a form of carefully placed protection (stop losses).

OPENNESS

You don't even want to get me started talking about how open-minded my father is. The whole family knows this and has learned to live with it. We still love him just the same, despite his tendency to be wide open and prone to some pretty fanciful, wild, and occasionally even crazy ideas. Trust me: We did not need the NEO-AC to tell us that Dad is off the charts in openness. But just for the record, his total openness score is a flabbergasting (O = 163). Professionally speaking, that is the highest total O score I have ever come across. While he did not max out on any of the individual O facets (as he did on two of the E facets), keep in mind that extreme scores in one of the five main personality domains (N, E, O, A, or C) are generally going to be more relevant than extreme scores on any single facet.

LARRY: My view is that this is correct. And I never really realized just how extreme in the openness trait I am, until I saw the results of my personality test, but it sure helped explain a lot of things in my life. I think it's a two-edged sword. I have been burned by being so open, but it has also allowed me to open doors and to have experiences in life that others would have shied away from. For example, I have studied all sorts of market theories because of this open door policy, ranging from the most serious to the most oddball and eclectic ideas. I have always been willing to explore anything and everything that might in some way contribute to my understanding of the markets. Don't laugh, but I have even studied lunar patterns to markets—and have even found some genuine usefulness there!

Not only does he score very high in fantasy (O1), aesthetics (O2), feelings (O3), and ideas (O5), but when it comes to the openness facet that most relates to risk aversion, actions (O4 = 20), his score is also relatively high. It's not off the charts high, but it is certainly high, higher than that of many other stocks and commodities traders I have studied. Remember, a high O4 indicates a trader who is a risk-taker for the purpose of fulfilling "greedy" desires (wanting to make money and be afforded the privileges that money can offer).

But what about Dad's other risk taking facets—the ones that are associated with taking risks more for the thrill and excitement of it? He scores high in these facets, as well (N5 = 19, E5 = 21). The combination of these NEO-AC risk-taking scores (especially E5 and O4) really goes to show that my father is all around a *huge* risk-taker. And, sure enough, he will be the first one to tell you that he likes trading (back to that earlier surfing analogy) the "big waves."

LARRY: You only live once. I want to experience this life to its fullest. And in the end, it will all work out for the better, one way or another. That has always been my life's mantra.

In fact, when discussing this with Dad in detail, I find that he has even convinced himself that the only way to make decent money in the markets is to hitch a ride on the giant swings in the market. He believes that trying to catch multiple medium-sized trades is not going to be profitable in the long term. His rationale is that there are bound to be huge losses along the way, and the only way to make up for them is to have some really huge gains. So he is always on the lookout for the major moves in markets.

Is he right? Is catching and then staying on the big swells the only way to make money trading the markets? Well, yes and no. For himself he is indeed correct, and he should not try to change this outlook because it works well for him. He would likely get bored and lose focus trading small moves in the market, and the end result would likely be failure. But I have talked to very successful market traders who are terrified of riding out the big bull and bear runs. These traders are much more content and comfortable with pinpointing more modest turns in the markets and taking a quick profit on each one, before any potential intratrade volatility starts to freak them out. And of course, with this more conservative trading philosophy, these lower-risk traders are less likely to sustain huge hits and drawdowns, so they don't need monster trades to save their day.

> Larry: I still contend that small-profit traders don't last long. This has nothing to do with personality, but the math of investment. I have written about that.

Keep in mind, of course, that everything is relative. A "small-profit trade" to my dad may look like a medium-profit trade to someone else who is more risk averse or vice versa. Very few futures traders are going to be low in the trait of risk-taking. In fact, my dad is a bit of an anomaly compared to most of the other successful traders I tested and interviewed for this book. Most of them had either average or only slightly elevated risk-taking tendencies.

One more thought about my father's incredible degree of openness. Appendix B discusses personality styles and how to determine them. The way you do this is to plot the most extreme scores for the big five traits (N, E, O, A, and C) against one another. In my father's case, the two domains that he had extreme scores in were very high E and O. If you turn to the "Style of Interests" section of Appendix B and read the description of O+, E+ (right upper quadrant page 203), you will basically be reading a very accurate description of who my dad is at his core!

AGREEABLENESS

The agreeableness (A) scale probably has less relevance for traders than for the others, but for completeness' sake I will not skip over how my father fared here. In particular we will see how the confluence of A with other traits speaks loudly about who my dad is.

First, he scores in the very high range on trust (A1 = 29). This level of trust in others, in combination with his incredible degree of openness (especially O5, ideas) leaves him wide open to abuse and manipulation at the hands of others. The markets themselves are not able to take advantage of such a gullible and naive individual, as the markets do not have a mind of their own. But my father is very susceptible to being taken advantage of by shrewd and cunning people. Hence, you may have heard about my father's little IRS troubles he got into after he followed the advice of some very disreputable and exploitive tax advisors. You can read about it in his book, *Confessions of a Radical Tax Protestor*.[1] In this case, his eventual fight with the IRS (which he won, by the way) probably diverted a lot of his attention from his two true passions in life: trading the markets and spending time with his family. There was probably a big legal bill at the end of the day, too. So although his high levels of openness and trust may not have directly affected his trading lifestyle, certainly they did indirectly.

> LARRY: It cost me several million dollars to become aware of all of this, and even then I did not see that my willingness to trust was a large weakness. I needed to become aware of that. A long-time secretary that I trusted like a member of our family embezzled over $1,000,000 from right under my nose. Then, I was lead into the "tax resistance" community by a great friend and lawyer that I just assumed knew what he was talking about. I also followed the advice of some CPAs because they worked for Big-Eight firms. I tossed away several million dollars in bad investments, simply because I trusted people I knew too much. At times I even did big business deals on nothing but a gentleman's handshake and with no contracts to back it up. Nowadays, I trust but verify. In fact, just recently somebody I deeply respect and admire presented me with a very tempting business opportunity. I was ready to push my chips all in, but then took a step back, realizing this was a similar pattern to that which had spelled disaster for me in the past. Had I not known of this aspect of my personality, I likely would have lost a sizable amount of money. So I guess it really does pay to get to know your personality.

On the straightforwardness facet my father scores very low (A2 = 13). This score indicates that he can be very clever and use circuitous or oblique ways to mentally solve problems. His mind can operate well in nonlinear thought patterns. So it is an interesting combination: he is someone who is mentally agile, but at the same time he is someone who is subject to being taken advantage of by the shrewd.

People who are very low on the A2 scale have the propensity to be "pathological" —but only when this score is also seen in conjunction with low scores on a number of other telling facets. For example, if my father were also low in A3 (altruism), A4 (compliance), and substantially lower on a number of the conscientious facets, I would caution you about doing business dealings with him. As it turns out, though, he is high in altruism and compliance. So instead of this being a negative trait, his cleverness is much more of an adaptive and healthy trait that he can apply to solving complex puzzles. I suspect this is why he has developed innovative and creative market approaches, systems, and indicators, not just once, but for many years.

CONSCIENTIOUSNESS

Dad scores in the average range on the overall conscientiousness scale (C = 126). Interestingly, though, there are two conscientiousness facets in which he scores very low: C2 (order) and C6 (deliberation).

Now, I am probably about to reveal a personal secret about Larry Williams that many of you may never have known. Larry Williams, the great inventor of technical indicators (%R) used throughout the world, and Larry Williams the discoverer of some very powerful trading systems (Oops!), is really *not* a systems trader!

Sure, he uses indicators and systems, but not nearly as much as you may think. When I watch my dad trade, I am amazed by two things: (1) how disorderly his trading desk is (sorry dad, but I have to reveal this purely in the interest of research), and (2) he often trades by hunches.

Okay, he doesn't really trade the markets on hunches; that's of course an exaggeration thrown in to try to provoke a reply out of him. Because it's not that there is no logic, rhyme, or reason to his trading style; obviously there is a huge amount of that. His trades are well educated, well researched, well calculated, and are even *based on* multiple systems and indicators. But, by and large, he is not truly trading via systems. There is not a master formula instructing him when to buy or sell a given commodity. Even with fancy computer software constantly helping him assess the current market situation, for the most part he prefers to reserve for himself the final judgment about if and when he is going to place a trade. His computers help him, indeed, but in the end he makes the call, not some software system. And he does so based on what he visually sees on his charts and monitors. It is a collective hodgepodge of data and indicators that he is constantly sifting through and sorting out, trying to decide when to get in or out of the markets.

Dad has commented to me many times that, when he tries to precisely follow his own systems or patterns, he usually fails in making money, even though some of his students, who are probably higher in C, will be very profitable doing just that, using *his* systems!

> LARRY: Of course I don't trade on hunches. But it is also true that I am not a strict systems trader. I see trading as an art that requires certain tools. I have tools that I use to set up trades, tools that tell me when and where to enter a trade, and tools that tell me when and where to exit a trade. I never feel as though a trade is going to be a big winner without having done some research that backs up the idea. To me a hunch is like an internal feeling, a voice whispering in the cobwebs of your mind or perhaps a sense of urgency to take this trade. I simply never feel that way. I know why I am putting on all my trades, and anyone who understands my work can agree.

My father is a great pattern analyzer. Probably his most proficient technical ability is in spotting market patterns in the here and now and deciphering what, if anything, they mean. His average to low C facets, along with a very high level of artistic creativity (his O1 and O2 scores are both sky high) and cleverness (very low A2), indicate that he is ideally suited to this style of trading. In particular, being low in C2 means that he will struggle trying to conform to a set of trading rules that he has to follow, regardless of what he really thinks or sees is developing in a market.

Dad is a very visual person: He sees symmetry and asymmetry, and he spots patterns far better than most of us. This is his strength. He will look at a given market chart up close and then roll his chair back away from his screen four or five feet and get a totally different perspective of exactly the same chart. But, when it comes time to making trades, he is generally not following systems. Larry Williams the great systems trader is, for the most part, a myth. Larry Williams is a great *patterns* trader.

> LARRY: Like I said, to me trading is a form of art. But as to this point, son, you bring up a very valid issue. The irony of it has always amused and confused me. I would like to think that I have done some very creative market work, such as in the development of my Ultimate Oscillator, Valuations measures for futures, Synthetic Vix Index, and all the work I have done on the Commitment of Traders Report. Then there is the work I did with Tom DeMark developing Sequential, one of the most interesting techniques you will ever see. On top of that, I have developed many, many powerful trading systems of my own that never took on names or gained notoriety beyond being shared with some of my students. But the funny thing is I could never follow the damned things. The day-to-day mundane details of following a system are just not what I am cut out to do. I'd far rather do more research or just trade using my own "art of trading" strategy. For me, trying to religiously trade and follow a system is a fight I can never win. Why? Because I am only fighting myself, my own personality traits, when I do that. I have come to learn why that is a shoe that just does not naturally fit and never will. Thus, I can make a direct and conscious choice to not follow systems, even the ones I create, and learn to be OK with that. Or, I can follow systems, but in doing so, realize that I have to adapt to my "self" and be judicious in that task, as it is one that I tend to shirk.

Linda Raschke, when being interviewed for this book, told me a funny story: "Your dad once told me he was the best systems trader in the world. I asked him how he did it, since I am a discretionary trader. He said that the only way he could do it was to put a copy of the system on the desk of one of his trading buddies. He had his buddy trade it for him while he went off to fish the remote streams of Montana because he could not stand watching his money stuck in a system!"

I think it is clear that, over the years and decades, my father has adapted his trading style and methods to match his unique set of personality traits. Through trial and error, and probably with some painful lessons along the way, he has been able to figure out what works best for him. For him it comes down to identifying unique patterns and trends in the markets, waiting for the big move, high-risk trades, and controlling his losses with very carefully placed stops.

Mental Edge Tips

LARRY: The personality assessment's greatest value, as I see it, is to help us create the trading style that best suits our individual temperaments and gives us an in-depth understanding of how to deal with risk. Lastly, it allows us to appreciate our personality traits as a whole and regulate them as needed when it comes to losing streaks or winning streaks (both in the markets and in other areas of our lives).

CHAPTER 23

Personality Case Study: Dan Zanger

Dan Zanger's biggest (though certainly not only) claim to fame in trading the stock markets came when—in a little less than two years—he turned a little less than $11,000 into $18 million. That's a mind boggling 164,000 percent in profit! Sounds more like lottery playing than market trading, right? This feat is widely regarded as the world record for the largest percent change for a personal portfolio in any stock market for either a 12-month or an 18-month period of time.

This staggering performance landed Dan on the cover of several magazines, such as *Fortune, Forbes*, and *Stocks & Commodities*. And in a business where many traders make bold or unsubstantiated claims and tell exaggerated "fish stories," Dan backed it up by showing *Fortune Magazine* his 1999 tax returns and trading records indicating that it was all true!

Dan Zanger grew up in the San Fernando Valley area of Los Angeles. His father was a physician, whereas his mother was a psychologist. He dropped out of college and moved to the Rockies to try snow skiing for a few years. Next, he had a few odd jobs, such as bellhopping, driving a cab, and working as a prep cook. None of these did he find adequately satisfying.

Eventually Dan moved back to LA—with no education and no profession or trade to call his own. He started working for a landscape company and eventually got his own independent contractor's license. Building swimming pools in Beverly Hills, he made a modest living. He wanted more challenge and more freedom.

Dan's mother, Elaine, loved the stock market, and he would often watch the business channel on TV with her, fascinated by the workings of Wall Street. One day in 1978, Dan saw a stock explode across the ticker crawl at the bottom of the screen. He made his first stock purchase, at $1, and sold the stock a few weeks later for a little over $3. Although the profit from that one trade was rather miniscule, he was enticed by the idea of a huge percentage gain in a brief period of time. He started dabbling in stocks on the side to begin with and eventually went on to get out of the swimming pool business and become a full-time trader. With the personal computers and trading software programs coming onto the scene in the late 1970s and early 1980s, Dan found that he was able to quickly review hundreds of charts in a single night in preparation for his next day's trading. For the next several decades Dan had his share of winning streaks.

Dan was, of course, a successful trader both prior to and following his incredible 18-month run. He just wasn't a "household name" in the trading industry. Today he is, and Dan Zanger is widely followed by traders around the world in his "Zanger Report"—a newsletter that assists others in trading, based on his use of charts. He makes no bones about it: Charts are all that matter in his trading decisions.

Dan is also the first to admit that the astronomical profits he made during the peak of the tech bubble may never be repeated again. But he continues to be a very profitable and reliable trader. Trading is still his primary source of income, and he trades only for himself. He spends over 70 hours per week trading or researching trades and on average takes around 10 to 20 positions in the stock market per week. His average trade is intermediate in duration (5 to 30 days). And although Dan relies heavily on charts and indicators to help pick his stocks, he uses discretionary trading and not mechanical systems to pick entry and exit points. Interestingly, in our survey of top traders, Dan was the only one who felt that managing emotions was "very important" to having success at trading (all of the other traders rated it as "extremely important.")

What stands out most about Dan's NEO-AC results is that he actually has a high score on the anxiety facet (N1). Almost all of our big-league super traders had low or very low anxiety scores, and only a small handful had average anxiety. Only Dan and one other trader sported an elevated N1 score. So this was a curious finding, and one that certainly deserves attention—the thought being that, if Dan can be a successful trader with this unusual trait, others like him might be able to as well. In fact, hoping to learn the secrets of managing anxiety, I was more eager to talk to Dan about his high N1 anxiety score than I was to talk with the successful traders who consistently have a predisposition to low anxiety. Dan was an outlier and an oddity in our research, and so I wanted to find out what this was all about. Dan told me this:

> I am an anxious person. That is certainly true. I always have been. The way I get past my anxiety in the here and now of volatile markets is to look at the big picture. I use historical reference points in the markets, the big drops over the past 20 to 30 years. By doing this, I am better able to appreciate things. It helps me hold onto my winning positions during a minor correction. It puts it all into perspective. The temptation is to get out of and then back into the market at each anxious moment, when really what I should be doing is raising more cash to support my current position—if I really know, based on good information, that it is the right one.
>
> Also, anxiety of losing money has saved me many times. It helped me avoid many breaks in the market. So to me, I see my anxiety as a good thing. I have a clear understanding that the power of the markets can wipe you out in a heartbeat. I know that my anxiety may push me to reduce my positions quickly. But I also know at the end of the day I am going to have more wins than losses if I stick to my guns and what I think is really happening in the markets. And my bigger gains from making the right calls based on solid logic will compensate for the smaller losses I sustain from losses related to anxiety.
>
> I have no tolerance for slow-moving stocks. I am a swing trader, not an investor. And I am clear on what I do. I pick my spots. I wait for the right setup. This forces me, an anxious person, to be more patient. As I am sitting there, looking at a stock, trying to figure out if I should hold it or fold it, I go through this very cognitive process. But I think that my anxiety has allowed me to hone my skills of knowing what is going on in the behind-the-scenes games that are being played on Wall Street.

Some people who follow my trading think I am psychic. They think I must have some mystical power to be ahead of the curve so often in the markets. But I think it's really part of my anxiety. It's almost a degree of being paranoid, although I don't know if that's the best choice of words for your book! Of course I'm not really paranoid. What I mean is that my anxious trait allows me to really read the markets and be in tune with them. It's hard to explain what I mean, but it's like I have a better pulse on the markets because of it. So I have learned to use it.

Dan scores low on the order facet of conscientiousness (C2). The clear trend with successful traders is this: Low scores in C2 correlate with traders who employ discretionary trading methods to make money, while high scores in C2 invariably are linked to traders who turn to mechanical systems to dominate the markets. Sure enough, Dan describes himself as a discretionary trader:

> I am always looking for a stock that screams, "Buy me!" I look at the fundamentals—its earnings, if it's in a popular group, whether or not it's overextended or even over-sold. But in general, as an individual investor I want to be the fly on the back of the pachyderm. When the pack moves, I want to be traveling right along with it, going in the right direction, basically going along for the ride. So I am very selective about which pachyderm I land on and when. From my perspective, mechanical patterns never get you very far. I am looking for that big explosive swing in the market, and the only way I know how to do that is to use discretionary methods, looking for the ripe moment when the pack busts out. Systems can't predict that.

Dan also commented on his slightly high excitement-seeking (E5) score:

> I am a thrill seeker by nature. But I also know that the markets are here to take your money and not to make you money. It's just like a casino in that sense. The casino was built to take your money, and so too was the market. That's just the cold reality of it. Reminding myself of that fact helps me to put the brakes on and helps me make sure that I am not getting into the markets just for a thrill. It forces me to be very careful about when to buy a stock. I have to be very calculated and disciplined. Otherwise I could easily get caught up in the latest market craze. I see myself as an "ice cold trader," and I try to keep things black and white and be methodical in what I do; I force myself to take the emotional thrill out of it. But at the same

time, inside I know I love the thrill. I always liked thrills. As a kid I liked fast cars, and that's why I liked speed skiing.

When I was working in the swimming-pool business and first learned how to spot a hot stock, and especially predict increasing valuation of stock, it was a thrilling experience. In fact, I think it's brought a real freedom to my life, and it's become my passion, that thrill of picking winning stocks. It really has been a life of freedom. I don't have to take care of retail customers, worry about overhead, getting sued by customers, or suing customers just to get paid. I find it a thrill to be in my own little world and not at the mercy of anyone else. I'm no longer subservient to anyone.

But I know I have to keep my thrill-seeking under wraps. At one point in the past my thrill-seeking nature resulted in a huge loss in the markets. I went flat broke when tech stocks were cut in half and I was 50 percent margined. It took the huge hit in 1997 for me to realize that trading is a very serious business. I need to always remember that, otherwise my thrill-seeking comes out. and I know I will lose money if it does. I think I learned my lesson, and because of it, today I am more careful about the thrill-seeking aspect of trading.

CHAPTER 24

Personality Case Study: KD Angle

Prior to his life as a trader, KD Angle (a.k.a. Kelly Angle) had a busy life. He attended both Wichita State University and the University of Southern California and graduated with a degree emphasizing political science and psychology.

KD used to have "real jobs." Before entering the trading arena, he worked as an operations officer in a diversified firm that was active in oil and gas exploration, drilling rig contracting, refining of special gases, a cattle feeding operation, two regional banking institutions, commercial real estate holdings, and the ownership and operation of a luxury hotel. Busy guy!

It was from this business experience, which involved working closely with related commodity interests, that KD was introduced to trading the futures markets. He entered the futures industry in 1985, with a newsletter and hotline advisory service known as the Timing Device; it was reported in *Forbes* magazine as being the number one commodity futures newsletter in 1986. He began managing assets in the futures markets shortly thereafter.

KD has also authored several books on trading. KD's *One Hundred Million Dollars in Profits (An Anatomy of a Market Killing)* gives his account of a trading experience that influenced his decision to give up his day job and commit his career to the trading industry.[1] KD's unique views on the markets and trading strategies have been published in nationally respected publications such as

Stocks and Commodities Magazine and *Futures Magazine.* He has also been interviewed on the CNBC business television network for his opinions on the markets.

KD was first registered as a Commodity Trading Advisor in 1986. He also serves as CEO and founder of a couple of companies registered as Commodity Trading Advisors with the Commodity Futures Trading Commission.

Currently KD runs two highly successful managed-futures investment programs. The older of the two is the Genesis Program, and the other is the Keck Program. Both are fully systematic in their trading methods.

How successful is KD? Well, the Genesis Program began in 2000 and has generated a compounded average rate of return of 16.83 percent. The Keck program began in 2003 and has generated a compounded average annual rate of return of 19.95 percent. If you add it up, that's a total return of 546.41 percent and 355.49 percent, respectively. In comparison, the S&P 500 total return index, over the same time period had a total return of 17 percent. If one thing can be said about KD's documented results, it's that he has been very, very consistent over the years.

True to form, KD scores high in total conscientiousness (C) and in particular on the order facet (C2), indicating that his personality is better suited to systems trading as opposed to discretionary trading. As such, KD describes spending less than 10 hours per week (not per day, per week!) trading the markets. He takes fewer than 5 positions per week, and he describes his trading positions as "long term"—over 30 days. KD had the following to tell us:

> I trade systematically and have employed the same two exact trading systems since 2000 and 2003, and have not made a material change to them since inception of trading. Because they are 100 percent systematic, I can delegate the process, and I have for years. My expertise is not in having the personality of a trader, but in doing good research in system design. This is the true art of trading. I believe it separates the men from the boys over the long haul. I compete against some of the most well-educated computer and math PhDs in the country, and my point is this: A system that consistently ends up in the top tier of performance is created from good design and disciplined execution. This is the reason for this success. I would also say that my work ethic has more to do with conducting the best possible research and design results, rather than from having superior intelligence.

I also believe that trading over many years has had an influence on my personality. For example, because I have no expectation about the results of a trade when I put it on, I am fairly expectation-neutral about all actions in my life. I didn't start out this way. Some say half of life is expectation, but I would say my expectation factor in most things that I do in life is fairly tempered, with a "wait and see" emotional response. This is a result of my trading. I do not believe that a person is born to trade; like most skill sets, it can be learned over time when taught to the person who is motivated enough to learn what is required to succeed.

Most people who trade do not really trade for the money. They think they are trading for money, but in reality it has more to do with other things. I think amateur traders tend to use trading as a distraction from their day jobs, with the hope of changing their current life condition into something more desirable.

Did you hear what KD said? "I have no expectation about the results of a trade." In fact, this was a consistent theme we heard over and over while interviewing top market traders. They also frequently make reference to "not doing it for the money." Now of course every trader wants to make money trading. After all, real money is at stake, and nobody wants to lose real money. But the successful trader's mind is not so preoccupied with the concept of mega-riches around each and every next turn in the market that she can't function. By learning to take a more guarded "wait and see" approach, she can concentrate more on the actual art and skill of trading, or in KD's case understanding what is required when it comes to designing trading systems that actually perform in the markets. Greed, which undoubtedly we all have to one degree or another, is not controlling the actions of superior traders.

In a sense greed is the opposite emotion to anxiety or fear. Greed is the emotion that makes us do things, while fear is the emotion that slows us down or stops us from doing things. The right amount of greed is of course necessary. Greed provides us with the motivation to work hard at something and do a good job at it. In fact, the concept that material wealth can measure happiness, fulfillment, and success is propagated throughout our society. Almost from the time you are born, you are taught the value and influence of money.

However, when we are too greedy, we start to take actions (remember, we are looking at the O4 facet here) that otherwise we would not. It's that lust for just a little bit more. In market trading, greed can make traders enter random or poorly thought out trades. Greed can cause you to hold onto positions longer than your trading system dictates or your better judgment would usually allow. Greed is the emotion that causes many traders to buy a stock or futures contract right at the end of the up move, or makes them hold onto a position just a little bit longer than they should, hoping to squeeze a few more points out of it. Have you ever caught yourself thinking, "Wow, this thing is going up fast! I'm going to get in right now!" It is only after you get into the trade that you recognize that the trend has already started to exhaust itself and has begun to reverse. This is a classic case of greed, perhaps mixed in with impulsivity.

A very profitable trading day can easily be lost in one instance of greed. Every individual has different triggers that often lead back to an underlying attachment to money. One of the most effective approaches to combating greed is to understand why it exists and to identify when it happens in your trading. But, from our research and interviewing of successful traders, it may be even more important to delete the idea that the almighty dollar sign defines your happiness and success in life or in trading. Here's another quote from KD to see where his happiness in being a trader lies:

> I receive more satisfaction from designing quality trading strategies than from the actual implementation of the strategy itself. Making a living from the markets is the business objective, and ultimately, if I couldn't earn a living from the markets, I would certainly do something else. But the design process is what I am most passionate about in this work.
>
> It is extremely difficult to create a market strategy that can perform well over many years when compared to an entire industry that is made up of some very bright and ambitious people. Knowing this gives me a great deal of satisfaction. But I also know that any strategy does not have to continue to perform well in the future just because it has done well in the past. I shy away from being too confident about future performance because I believe there is no place in this business for too much confidence. It can only blind one's ability to see clearly what is being employed in the markets. Like most aspects of this life, one cannot hope to obtain enough clarity when it comes to solving problems and making decisions.

CHAPTER 25

Personality Case Study: Linda Raschke

Linda Raschke began her full-time professional trading career in 1981, as a market maker in equity options. She began on the floor at the Pacific Coast Stock Exchange and later moved to the Philadelphia Stock Exchange. Although Raschke is probably best known as a short-term S&P 500 futures trader, she is actually active in several time frames, markets, and trading styles.

From 1982 to the present, Linda has been an independent, self-employed trader of equities, options, and futures. Since 1993 she has been a CTA (commodity trading advisor) trading futures. She has also managed commercial hedging programs in the metals markets. As a CTA she currently manages the Granat Fund. In 2009 Granat was ranked as the seventeenth best in terms of five-year performance, out of 4,500 hedge funds by BarclayHedge.

Linda breaks her trading down like this: 45 percent day trading, 45 percent short-term trading (2 to 5 days), and 10 percent intermediate trading (5 to 30 days). She spends on average 50 to 60 hours devoted to trading the markets each week, and during an average week she makes about 30 to 50 trades in the markets.

In our studies of highly successful traders, we found low anxiety (N1) and low vulnerability (N6) to be the norm. Linda exemplifies this point. She scored in the very low range on both of these N facets. These were the only two N facets that she scored in the very low range. We asked her about this.

Since I was young, I was very good at being single-minded and focused. My mom often accused me of being emotionally aloof and distant. From a young age I was very independent, being the oldest of four children, and learned to be self-sufficient early on. I had a very thick skin. I think one is born with these kinds of aspects. And I have learned that I have to be careful on the other end of the extreme from what most traders face. I have to take care to not be too emotionally down-regulated. It's probably beneficial to be a bit on the edge; it adds intensity. But I have to work on it; I have to take care not to be totally shut down emotionally. To be honest, I am very conscious of it.

There is always discussion and even debate among traders and psychologists as to whether women make better traders (or not), and if so, why so. Our research was not designed to directly answer this question per se. What it was designed to do, however, was assess whether the same traits that make for a successful male trader also make for a profitable female trader. The answer from our set of data seems to be yes—that low neuroticism (especially when it comes to the components of anxiety and vulnerability) is what matters most, regardless of whether you have one or two X chromosomes.

Keep in mind that the NEO-AC assesses the same 30 facets of personality in both men and women, and both genders answer exactly the same questions on the NEO-AC test. Historically speaking, large population data show that there are some differences in personality between the sexes (no kidding!), and it's for this reason that the adult norm scores on the NEO-AC are separate for men and women (the test has a scale for women and a scale for men). The main difference between the genders is that women tend to be somewhat more neurotic (N) and more agreeable (A) than men. It is noteworthy that Linda, a successful trader, fits the "perfect trader" personality profile, as one would expect from any great trader, male or female. Bottom line: Linda scores very low on both the N1 and N6 facets, her gender notwithstanding.

Our findings, that low N1 and N6 are vital to successful trading, may in fact indicate that men, at least based on personality traits alone, have the upper hand at successful trading, though certainly this still needs to be studied more, and I am not going to utter another word, over fear of putting my foot in my mouth!

Next, Linda has a low C2 score, which again indicates she would be well suited to the life of a discretionary trader. Here is what she had to say about it:

I started trading on the floor of the stock exchange. There was no such thing as mechanical trading down there—it was always so dynamic and ever-changing. But it was also tedious at times being down there. Some people think floor trading is glamorous. It's not. Sure, there were some good days, even super good days. But there were a lot of boring days and days filled with grief as well. I traded on the floor for five years until I had an accident and hurt my shoulder. At that point I could no longer trade on the floor. So I started trading from upstairs at my clearing firm and eventually transitioned to trading from my house. But all the while I remained a discretionary trader, since we did not have computers when I first started trading.

Things were pretty primitive when I first started trading from home. I had always subscribed to Security Market Research charts when I was on the floor and used to update the charts by hand as well as plot the daily oscillator readings. But I was also an excellent tape reader and good at monitoring the market internals. I was very much hands-on from the get-go.

Very few systems hold up over time. Most will deteriorate. If they didn't, everyone would be trading them. Two that I do believe in are volatility breakout systems and trend following systems. Unfortunately it is difficult to move much size on volatility breakout systems, and trend following approaches can have steep drawdowns—well beyond what I can. So I don't like trading systems. I never have.

Linda's words make an interesting contrast from what KD Angle had to tell us (see preceding chapter), how he has used the same two trading systems for many years without having to tweak them once. This really goes to show that you have to match your trading style to your personality and that trading is not one size fits all!

Here is what Linda has to say about her motivations and reasons for trading the markets:

I don't sit there and look at the money side of it. I know intuitively if I am up or down for the day, or maybe the month. But I have always found that I do better trading the markets if I do not keep looking at my performance. It's odd, because what I teach other traders is to have careful record-keeping skills and to monitor their profits and losses carefully. I did this diligently for the first 12 years I traded, but now I don't pay as much attention to the money side because I just know intuitively. I try to stay focused on the process instead. I can remember once in the spring of 1987 looking at new highs in my P and L and feeling pleased, and it ended up being the kiss of death as I did not take out those equity highs for another six months. New highs in the P and L lead to complacency and dropping of the guard so I learned that for me it only counts when it is the end of the month.

Actually, I think this makes perfect sense for Linda, given her low C facet scores. She goes on:

> I think I trade because I wouldn't know what else to do. I have no other skills, really. I wouldn't know how to make a living doing anything else other than trade. Also, it is fun to play a game when you know you can win at it on a regular basis. When I was 10 years old, I always won at Monopoly, so I liked playing Monopoly. The same thing goes with trading. I am good at it, so I like to do it.

I asked her if mastering the markets is an important concept to her, as it is to many of the other traders I talked with. Her reply:

> No, I don't think that's quite it. Although I want to master the markets, another side of me says I'll never really be able to master them. Let me put it this way: I have noticed that my ability to focus while trading has diminished a bit compared to 15 years ago. I have had a lot more distractions the past few years. I know the game of trading better than I ever did when I was younger, but I find that today the markets are 24/7 with global capital flows and thus are more demanding. Right now my challenge is to keep my mental edge sharp and keep up with my prior performance. That's my motivation for trading today.

On some other telling facets of the NEO-AC (O1, O2, O3, O5, and E6), Linda scores either high or very high. What we have found from interviewing traders is that being able to take in multiple concepts, sort them out, make sense of them, and apply them to the markets are very important. This multitasking and amalgamating of various concepts and applying them to a rapidly changing system, such as a stock or futures market, is what it takes. And it is especially huge for discretionary traders like Linda. (For instance, as you may recall, we saw this same pattern in my father's personality profile.)

> I think I have an ability to pick up on the concepts of historical figures and put them in terms that other people can relate to and make use of. I think I have a real skill there. I feel that I have come up with a lot of original concepts pertaining to price behavior as well.

Combining her N and O scores, Linda is a prime example of how the best investors/traders are able to multitask under pressure, all the while managing their emotional urges. Even though they may hold a particular trading style or philosophy, which they remain consistent with, they remain open to new ideas and adaptation. They are comfortable with change and improvisation and are always looking to expand on trading concepts.

CHAPTER 26

Personality Case Study: Andrea Unger

Andrea Unger spent nearly a decade working as a middle-level manager for a major Italian corporation. Although he enjoyed putting his mechanical engineering degree (from the University of Milan) to use in the workplace, he never cherished the harsh realities of corporate management.

> I had 30 people working under me, and I saw how people can be treated like numbers. The maneuvers I saw in business were sad, because you were dealing with people, and people have stories and families and lives. Top management would come in with directions to reduce here, to move people there. This is normal to meet the objectives of a company. I understand that it must be like that. But it's not what I like.

Andrea decided to move his life in a new direction in 2001. He set his sights on a career as a market trader. He sought advice from famed Italian trader Domenico Foti and soon became a top protégé and a very good trader. In late 2004 he attended a Larry Williams Million Dollar Challenge and has been a student and colleague of my dad's ever since.

> I look at everything, but I always try to adapt it to my personal way of trading. I look for ideas that should generate new ideas following my own style. I had two important people in my learning curve. One is an Italian friend, Domenico Foti, whom I started developing strategies

with early on. He is one of the best traders I know, and his support was very important—maybe not properly to teach, but rather to be a valid referral to discuss results and to gain confidence in what I was doing. The second guy is your father, Larry Williams. His job led me to become confident that it could really be done. I'm not using strategies of Larry, but I like his approach and his way to study markets. And his most important message is that there is always something new to be discovered and that we have to be ready to figure that out!

Andrea has an inquisitive mind, and he thirsts to learn and adopt the ideas of others. Yet he retains the ability to remain an independent trader and has artfully developed his own style of trading instead of just copying the moves or following the styles of others. It has paid off for him big time. His trading profits have skyrocketed, and his accomplishments and accolades have accumulated over the past decade as he established himself as one of Europe's best traders. He won the futures trading title in the 2005 Top Trader Cup competition, sponsored by LombardReport.com. One year later Andrea published *Money Management: Methods and Applications*, the first Italian-language book on money management for traders. A member of Mensa, Andrea also won a month-long IW Bank "T Cup" trading contest with a 50 percent gain in that single month.

Unger fulfilled a dream and went on to worldwide acclaim in trading by winning the 2008 World Cup Championship of Futures Trading, which he captured with a very hefty 672 percent net return at the end of the year. Proving it was no fluke, he recorded a 115 percent return in 2009 to become the first back-to-back winner of the competition in nearly 20 years. But he didn't stop there. Andrea went on to post a 240 percent return in the 2010 World Cup Championship, to pull off an unprecedented World Cup three-peat.

Andrea is a full-time trader who appreciates the complexities of the markets. "There is no easy money out there," he says. "Markets require discipline and application to be understood. I try to develop methods that apply to the markets. I never try to apply the market to my ideas."

When it came to Andrea's NEO-AC results, some interesting patterns emerged. But before we get started dissecting his personality, I want to thank Andrea for allowing me to use his name, NEO results and story, because as you are about to read, it is rather personal information. (In fact, we offered all the successful traders who took the personality test anonymity in this book, and many preferred to remain nameless, for obvious reasons.) The fact that Andrea was agreeable to our making public his personality traits and how they have affected his trading is a testimony to his desire to learn more about himself and how he can be an even more accomplished trader. So, Andrea, thanks again for giving back and allowing our readers to learn from you.

Overall Andrea's N score is quite average (78). But looking at this score by itself could be a bit deceiving and really goes to show that you have to take the full personality test, the one that breaks neuroticism down into its facets. Otherwise, one might think that Andrea is neither low nor high in emotional reactivity, when the truth is that he's a bit of a complex personality.

Andrea scored low on the anxiety (N1) facet and the vulnerability (N6) facet. Nothing much to write home about there: That's the pattern that we consistently saw in successful market traders. Meanwhile, on one of his neuroticism facets, N3 (depression), Andrea actually comes in quite high—and in fact his score is right on the verge of being very high. Nobody else in our group of traders had this score. Again, a high N3 facet does not mean that one is always sad or blue. It means that under certain stressful situations one is bound to feel reactive sadness more strongly than the average person. But not only did Andrea score high in N3, on the extraversion side of things, his E6 facet (positive emotions) was very low.

When I first reviewed these findings, prior to discussing them with Andrea, already certain thoughts were entering my mind. With such a personality makeup (high depression and very low positive emotions), one would have to be very careful about becoming excessively sad or gloomy in the setting of a bad move in the market. This kind of reactive sadness could easily interfere with the cognitive aspects of appropriately managing the next trade or scoping out the next turn in the market. Or depressed feelings stemming from other areas of one's life could equally impair one's trading. With this particular combination of traits, I would even have concerns that a spell of bad trades in the market could potentially send such an individual into a real spiral downward, and maybe even clinical depression—which would have huge consequences if not recognized early on and corrected through treatments.

When I shared with Andrea these "depressing" results of his personality profile, he was surprised at how insightful the test was. He told me that at times he does indeed experience substantial dips into sadness related to market trading. In fact, he revealed to me that he had recently been in a protracted state of relative unhappiness with his trading and that his trading results had suffered from it. He was no longer able to perform up to his old standards during this unhappy period, and this was new to him.

Digging deeper to uncover the source of his recent sadness, Andrea discovered that it set in, not because he himself was making bad trades or posting losses, but rather it occurred when other traders lost some of their moneyfollowing trading advice he had given them. You see, as Andrea gained notoriety (and deservedly so) as one of the world's most successful futures trader, a contingent of traders (likely high in dependency) tried to follow and emulate Andrea. As we discussed in the chapter on the overly dependent trader, trying to mimic the "gurus" of market trading is a surefire way *not* to succeed in this business of trading. Here is what Andrea told me:

> More than once I have opened positions in my own accounts that are against or contradict those that I recommend in my signal programs. That may happen due to different time frames or time horizons of the trades, or even because other systems open opposite trades on markets correlated to the signals.
>
> Well, most often I'm happy to lose money in those positions—hoping my "followers" are happy and gaining in their positions. This is a silly attitude, as both approaches are valuable in the medium to long term. But I have the feeling that I can support my own losses and *understand* them better than any of my followers. I know how delicate putting money into something is, so my main concern always remains with customer satisfaction. I have not found a solution so far, unfortunately. If a student of a seminar of mine or a fellow trader following some of my signal programs loses money, I really feel sorry about it.
>
> Feeling sorry does cause problems. My mood is bad. I may discretionarily "move from the system" that generates trades for the followers. Normally it is a mistake, I know. But that mistake comes back from time to time. I always look into the systems I use for followers trying to improve them and to solve issues related to losses. It does not reverse the feeling sorry, but it is a way to try to help.

As Andrea struggled with his emotional response to the reality of others losing real money after listening to and following his advice, it had an influence on his own trades.

> What I learned from my personality profile was much more than I expected, actually. I think you described things really in depth, and I recognized myself in what you pointed out. It is interesting how you found out the sad part of me in doing things. I usually don't care when my money is involved, but I feel the way you said when losses are harming people following me.
>
> This point about feeling "sorry" applies not only to students of mine but also, and even more heavily so, to my newsletter followers and to my advisor program followers such as World Cup Advisor Trades. In those cases, I simply am following systems whose trades I either publish in the newsletter or I place on my accounts. My followers get trades executed as well, through auto-trade tools. Obviously these kind of followers are totally dependent on me, not because of the way I treat or educate them, but simply because of the type of service they are purchasing. The service I provides leaves little or nothing to discretionary decision making. They obviously can choose to not follow the newsletter's indications or close the opened trades on their account—but that would probably be a silly behavior, having paid for that kind of service.

In Andrea's case, I really can see only two potential solutions to this problem of sadness in response to followers losing money following him. Either he has to learn how to turn down requests for advice (stop being a guru or a teacher and just trade for himself— although if he likes teaching, this is not an option), or he will have to learn to not take responsibility and blame for the mistakes or failures of traders who are too dependent upon him for advice. If people choose to trace every step of Andrea's in the markets, they do so at their own risk.

Just as Andrea became successful by blazing his own distinct trail with the guidance of several mentors and teachers, it's important for him to realize that now that he is the teacher, he too needs to guide his students to find their own styles and their own ways of market trading. He needs to remind students not to try and duplicate what he does, but to expand on it and adapt it to their own trading strategies. Maybe he needs to find ways to incorporate more discretionary trading into the services that he currently offers.

This may take time for Andrea to really appreciate. As a very independent trader who uses mentors and teachers wisely, he may not fully grasp that some of his followers really struggle with being overly dependent—all based on their personality traits. Of course, intellectually Andrea knows these people are too dependent on him and his trading advice, but he might not really see how shackled to it they are and might not see how easy it is to fall into the trap of providing them the advice they want to hear from him.

At that point it is a self-fulfilling prophecy: By feeding them explicit trading instructions or advice that their ears want to hear, Andrea is basically setting up some of his followers for failure in the markets, which in turn will make him sad, which in turn will have an effect on his own personal trading. Of course, some of his followers will use Andrea's services wisely and appropriately, learn to reap rewards from them, and go on to become fully independent, successful traders; some of his protégés will likely go on to become teachers themselves one day. Andrea just has to be aware that some followers will fail in trying to emulate him, and that when it happens, it is not his fault.

So it will be helpful for Andrea to fully take into consideration the dependency of others and how he may have to modify his teachings or trading advice to them. Ultimately, one way or other, I think that Andrea is going to have to incorporate into his trading advice the importance of his followers' learning how to be more independent themselves and not relying too heavily on him for success in the markets. Likely only then will Andrea be released from the sadness that he feels when his followers lose money.

This case example is unique and specialized for Andrea and likely does not directly apply to you. However, the point is that the results for the NEO-AC test can be very telling and helpful in trying to unwrap some of the emotional aspects of your trading and how it is holding you back from trading to your fullest potential.

Moving into the realm of conscientiousness, an oddity occurs in the personality results for Andrea Unger. Recall that successful traders who are low in the C2 facet (order) are, for the most part, trading the markets with discretionary methods, while those who are high in C2 usually trade with mechanic systems. This was *not* the case with Andrea; he is a systems trader who is low in C2. Trying to find out how this came to be, I asked Andrea about it.

I've been more successful with trading systems simply because I mainly used them. I feel more comfortable using systems, because the back test gives me more confidence in the coming trades.

This statement made me ponder. One can gain confidence from looking at the historical record of a system; that's very true. But, we also know that "past performance is no guarantee of future results." Also, from my discussions with other top traders, one can gain confidence looking at one's own historical record of picking winners. So does it come down to Andrea having more confidence in historical records than in his abilities? Well, it should be noted that Andrea's self-confidence as measured on the C1 (competency) facet of the NEO-AC test is slightly on the low side. This was also somewhat of an anomaly, compared to the scores of other successful traders, who generally had slightly elevated C1 scores, indicating stronger levels of self-confidence. I think this low C1 help explains why Andrea utilizes trading systems, despite being low in C2.

Obviously we would never suggest to Andrea that he overhaul his whole trading style and abandon systems trading after all the unparalleled success he has had. Don't fix what ain't broke! But at least this is some food for thought—and maybe even an opportunity for Andrea to step back and reassess why and how he trades. Andrea continues,

> To trade discretionary is a new challenge day after day, while using systems is more like an application of work that has already been done. The amount of stress I derive from trading (but also from any other activity) does not need additional day-by-day stress. And that's the main reason why I use systems. Yet there are periods where I place discretionary trades and, even though the total revenue of these is certainly positive, I don't even have precise figures about their results.
>
> Basically I don't like to be wrong, not because I don't want to lose, but because losing leads me to lose confidence as well. Using systems, the examination of it is extended to a longer time scale. A losing trade in a system is normal—a drawdown, too. I can judge if it as part of the system and if it could be expected or not. Discretionary trading is sort of challenging with every single trade, and there is no performance report. This leads to a verification process after every single entry and is harder to sustain.
>
> Another reason why I prefer systems is because they leave a certain degree of freedom during the day, as they trade automatically

and don't need my presence during the session. Yet, Jason, your response to me will not pass leaving no trace. I will consider it, and I will make up my mind if it is worth trying more discretionary trading. I just have to organize myself.

One final thought on why Andrea has gravitated to systems trading. Although low C2 was the primary trait found in successful discretionary traders, it was also common to see high scores on the O1, O2, and O3 and a low core on the A2 facet. See the chapters on my dad and Linda Raschke to read more about this. In Andrea's case, though, Andrea scores high in O1, but low in O2, and average in O3. And on the A2 score he scores very high. My point is that he may not have the personality trait profile to really appreciate the "art and beauty" of discretionary-style trading

CHAPTER 27

Personality Case Study: Ralph Vince

Over the past 30 years, Ralph Vince has worked with institutional asset management companies, managed millions of dollars, and advised both sovereign wealth funds and private traders. By profession Ralph is a computer programmer who writes analytical programs for funds, large traders, and professional gamblers. He is also the author of five books on investing in his field of expertise: portfolio management and portfolio/trade optimization.

Ralph Vince and my dad teamed up in 1987, when Pops took $10,000 to $1,110,000 to win the Robbins World Cup. Ralph was there as it happened, watching my dad employ the Kelly Ratio (more on this in a moment) for a very aggressive form of money management. Since then Ralph has developed into the premier expert on money-management systems for traders and investors. He has written numerous books (his latest title being *Risk-Opportunity Analysis*[1]) and professional papers on money management for trading, and introduced new statistical techniques that are in widespread use throughout the industry today. Ralph also conducts portfolio risk-management workshops for institutional portfolio managers. In 2011, the world's foremost index provider, Dow Jones Indexes, teamed up with Ralph's LSP Partners LLC to develop and co-brand an index family using a proprietary strategy created by Ralph.

In trading circles Ralph's name is virtually synonymous with strategic money management. But his story is even more interesting than that. In 1980, at the age of 20, Ralph went on his first job interview at a Paine Webber office in Cleveland, Ohio. Ralph was questioned as to whether he was there for the margin clerk job. Although he wasn't, he answered yes anyway, and started hard at work the next day as a margin clerk, despite having no formal financial education or training. However, what Vince did possess was an incredible ability in mathematics. As such, he was a brilliant margin clerk, as the job took advantage of Ralph's ability to quickly manually calculate margin requirements for short-option account positions. Ralph describes this initial work experience as "a baptism by fire and a great way to get started in the business."

But not satisfied with merely being a human abacus that made profits for others, Vince soon began trading his own money. And within several years he started working at a computer firm in New York that handled back-office processing for futures markets. Concurrently, IBM had just introduced the first personal computer. The industry was evolving into the modern era. But there was a problem. Traders could now buy computers, but there were no adequate software programs to help them actually put their computers to use! So it was only a matter of time before traders started knocking on Vince's door, pleading with him to design computer programs in order to rigorously test various trading strategies.

The next major milestone in Ralph's career came in 1985, when he first met my dad in the lobby of a Chicago hotel. A friendship was quickly struck, and at that point Williams asked Vince to test trading systems for him. "Larry was trading a lot of money at the time, and he opened my eyes in terms of money management and trading allocations."

Williams and Vince were both equally intrigued by Ed Thorp's treatise *Beat the Dealer*, which was first published in 1962.[2] In his book Thorp included formulas derived from the "Kelly criterion." These formulas examined how much a casino gambler should bet in order to maximize the expected value of his stake. There was only one problem. Thorp's formulas were initially meant to be used only in gambling scenarios, not in the markets. So Williams and Vince teamed up to tweak Thorp's formulas and then applied them to the markets.

It was a creative and brilliant application of Thorp's work. The formulas determine how much a trader should trade in order to maximize profits—based on his account's equity value as well as the perceived largest loss using a given trading system. Vince went on to publish this work in his book, *Portfolio Management Formulas*. He coined this money-management approach "optimal f."[3]

The bulk of market traders spend most of their time and energy on selecting the right market to trade, spotting a ripe setup, or developing the newest system or pattern than has historically been profitable. Ralph takes a different perspective. As one of the world's true gurus in money management, he is more diligent and devotes more time to thinking about his trading quantity (how much to trade). To him, strategic money management is more important than market selection and timing.

When I started my interview with Ralph, I initially only told him that his personality traits were remarkably different from those of the other traders we looked at under the microscope, but I didn't at first tell him what stood out in his trait profile. I wanted to get a raw, unbiased response to telling him that. He replied,

> Well, I am not surprised you say that. Trading for me has been a long and painful process, and I think this has to do with some shortcomings in my personality. I tend to be a skittish, flighty, and surface-minded person. These kinds of traits would work against most good traders. People who can focus have a clear advantage in the markets, and I don't have that going for me. It's the same in sports with the great athletes. Look at Manny Ramirez; guys like that can stand in the batter's box and be very relaxed, very fluid. They are able to get into that mental state very naturally. The good traders that I know are able to do the same thing, but I have a hard time with it. I tighten and stiffen up, and I can't focus on trading. I have really poor attention in this area. Look, the whole goal and purpose of trading is to make money, but when I am trading, I tend to forget that—I get easily distracted by other things, and it works against me.
>
> So over the years I had to come up with my own style that would be able to take this into account. That's why it was long and painful. And it's only been in the last three or four years that it's really become clear to me what that is—the whys are now known to me. What I found is that I need to make trading as boring as possible in order to make it work for me—to be profitable. Historically, that's where I make money, when what I am doing is as boring as a farmer watching his vegetables grow. When I am trading properly, it's boring and there is absolutely nothing gratifying about it. It's not

exciting, and it's not filling some void caused by my psychological shortcomings—either shortcomings that I'm aware of or maybe others that I'm not aware of! I really am "Mr. Boring Farmer" watching his crop grow.

It was at this point in my interview with Ralph that I brought up some of his personality traits. I mentioned that, of all the facets, his most extreme score was on the anger/hostility (N2) scale—on this dimension he almost scored off the charts. His second highest score, also in the very high range, is in assertiveness (E3). Keeping in mind the concept of "dimensions" (Chapter 4), the extreme scores are the most telling (either problematic or advantageous—think back to Yao Ming in Chapter 4!) and where we (psychologists and psychiatrists) turn our attention to first when formulating a client's personality as a whole. Besides Ralph, none of our other avant-garde traders had either one of these personality components (N2 or E3) in the high or very high range, so I was curious as to how they fit into his trading life. Ralph also scores high in anxiety (N1) and very high in impulsivity (N5). Keep in mind that, of the dozens of winning trader personalities we studied, only one other (that of Dan Zanger) was high in anxiety.

> Well (*jokingly referring to his wife*), let me tell you that there is someone in the next room who would concur on me having an angry streak! But seriously, it really goes right back to the boredom thing. When I was very, very young and just getting started in this business, it was an issue, such as revenge trading. But over time, I learned to channel this anger into positive trading. Via mathematics I was able to steer my anger emotion into something that was productive, and it helped me remain intensely focused. I used to do things that were self-destructive in the markets, even though I certainly did not want to be self-destructive. If a market I was in would go down in price suddenly and I was getting upset over it, I would buy more of it in a reactive emotional process, not because I really thought I should buy more. This was a long time ago, and this kind of emotional response has really dissipated over the years. I must have been awful back then!
>
> So what really works for me is to trade in a way that is so boring that it's even intolerable. It's funny—I remember when I was maybe 11 years old I was given some kind of personality test at school by a psychologist. I remember clearly when they called my name over

the PA system to go meet with the psychologist and discuss what the results were and meant. This psychologist explained to me that I was a very impulsive person and at high risk of abusing substances. Even now, 47 years later, I remember how serious this psychologist was at the time. It scared me. They were so concerned about me and my pathological personality, and I think I kept this in mind over the years.

In a sense, this conversation with you is huge. It really is clarifying to me what works for me and how I arrived at that. As long as I keep my trading style as boring as watching a vegetable garden grow, my anxiety and my anger and my impulsivity are kept under wraps. To me it means having my timing and selection work in a very systematic module. I only spend about 15 to 30 minutes per week trading, preparing for trades, or observing my trades. That's it. In fact, it's probably closer to 15 minutes per week, not 30. And I have found that the best trading in my life occurs when I stick to this method.

It took me time to figure this out, but by getting myself and my weaknesses out of the way, I can actually have crazy success in the markets, well beyond what I ever even imagined was possible. I used to be able to make money trading, but since I adopted this vegetable-garden method over the last three to four years, my success in trading has been virtually unstoppable. I can't emphasize this enough: I had to remove myself and any entertainment value from my trading.

I call it my "boredom program"—can you imagine that? Can you imagine if I had an infomercial on TV and tried to pitch my trading technique to others? "Now you too can have an incredibly boring job and life just like me!" It's almost comical, but this is my system, and it's what works for me.

I asked Ralph if he has ever or ever would manage money for others.

No. I would rather dig ditches than trade others' money. Really. Fortunately my system of trading has been integrated into a package of indexes that is marketed by Dow Jones, and this is nice because I know my work is out there, being used, and indirectly people can use me and my ideas to make money. But I would never want the job of trading the money of another person. You see, although it pales in comparison to the responsibility of a trauma surgeon who is operating on a dying patient or a lawyer who is defending someone in a murder trial, in a sense there is a lot of emotional responsibility in trading someone else's hard-earned money that I just don't think I would be able to handle.

You need to understand, my father was an extreme compulsive gambler. I grew up seeing how emotions operate in these kinds of realms. Imagine giving a gambler someone else's money to bet. When it's my money, I know what my own risks and expectations are. I wouldn't really know what someone else's trading criteria would be. They could be trying to fill some sort of psychological void by trading the markets, but by entrusting me to do it for them, the emotions are now mine, and not theirs, and it gets too tricky. If I gave them a 10 percent return, they might not be happy, even though for me 10 percent might be acceptable under certain market conditions.

Anyway, what I know is this. I really cannot afford to get tangled up in the web of human emotions—mine or someone else's. I have plenty of trouble tending to my own pathological tendencies, and I mean that seriously. I really can't take on someone else's.

Early on, I noticed that there was a "spectrum" of personality manifestations in the markets. There were the compulsive gamblers, the guys whose wives would come back to the cage and tell me, "You call me at this number if you see my husband trading options." Then there were the guys at the other end of the spectrum: the guys sitting in front of the tape, plotting out every little wiggly-jiggly of the market—and never putting on a trade!

And what I found is that the most important thing in trading is to first determine one's own criteria—what you are really doing it for. And armed with that, you aren't pulled in either direction on this spectrum—in fact, you aren't even *on* that spectrum once you know what you are seeking to accomplish, and the pursuit of those very criteria becomes necessarily boring. I have seen a direct correlation to how well-articulated one's criteria are and one's success in trading. Individual traders rarely have articulated criteria; successful institutions almost always do.

The day after my interview with Ralph, he sent me a very nice e-mail:

Thank you! I mean it—thank you so much. Our conversation last night led me to some insights I had not anticipated. Perhaps this is important for others.

I have discovered that the reason I am able to succeed at trading (despite being of a rather desperately tortive personality) is because

I was able to find a way to remove myself and my personality from it. I was able to extricate my personal panoply of psychological pathologies from the trading process entirely; to wit, I spend only 15 to 30 minutes a week at my job, if that. I came up with a process that intentionally avoids my inclusion. Because my success at this really is "extreme" in certain ways, I am thinking that it is exactly because I happened to be born with such screwed up traits that the path to removing them from impinging on my trading had to be that extreme. That's my boredom program, and it has lavished me with what it has.

None of this was entirely evident to me until after speaking to you last night. But it's starting to crystallize why I have been successful at this, and how I got there. I think you've pointed me in the direction of a great truth about all of this stuff, and I am very, very grateful.

CHAPTER 28

Personality Case Study: Scott Ramsey

Scott Ramsey has been trading the markets for over 30 years. He founded his company, Denali Asset Management, in 1994 and has been its president since its inception. Although hailing originally from Chicago, today Scott calls the U.S. Virgin Islands his home.

Scott runs Denali as a macro fund. He seeks to profit from broad economic trends by trading futures contracts on equity indexes, commodities, and currencies. Scott especially takes pride in being one of the few hedge-fund managers who survives and even thrives on turbulent market conditions. He says that his personal trading motto is: "From chaos comes opportunity." He notes that chaos occurs during a financial crisis as well as around significant economic reports and often coincides with trend changes.

Scott's performance has been amazing. During these hectic times he has never had a down year, and he now oversees over $1 billion worth of funds—all of which are traded exclusively in futures markets. Since the launch of Denali Partners L.P. in 2000, his average annual gain has been 16 percent. His worst monthly drawdown was only 10 percent.

Scott holds his trades for an average of a week or less, and he reports spending on average 50 to 60 hours per week trading or preparing for trades. He places about 20 to 30 traders per week. Scott is in the minority of professional hedge-fund traders in that he employs discretionary trading. As he puts it:

> I am a self-taught trader with an engineering background. At first I tried to write some of my own systems, and they did okay. Not great, but okay. It wasn't until I started reading and learning about the fundamentals of the market, though, that I started to make big money.
>
> I would never claim that either a systematic or discretionary methodology is superior to the other. I believe they are very different and each approach has its benefits and place in an investor's portfolio. I choose to manage assets as a discretionary CTA (commodity trading advisor), because it utilizes the skills I've developed trading on and off the exchange floor for over 30 years. The majority of the participants in the marketplace are traders who make their decisions based on expectations and emotions. Until such a time comes that computers can take over trading altogether, there will be a place for the discretionary trader who can sift through the emotion and act rationally when others aren't, identify the opportunities, and profit from them."

Not surprisingly, Scott scores low in C2 facet (order)—just like all of the discretionary traders we tested. A low C2 score basically predicts that a successful trader is using discretionary means to trade.

> Many of our clients and prospective clients have portfolios composed primarily of systematic CTAs that perform similarly during most market cycles. Our clients find value added in Denali's discretionary approach, because it complements their systematic CTAs and potentially smoothes overall portfolio performance during times of market turmoil.

As a prime example, Scott points to the financial crisis of 2008 and the ensuing "Great Recession." While many systematic CTAs were hemorrhaging money, Scott's Denali fund profited handsomely. Scott feels that his 30 years of trading experience combined with Denali's research and trading focus are the keys to its success. He acknowledges that chaos and wild market emotions during times of crisis can create opportunities to capitalize on—at least for those who are prepared and not caught focusing on losing trades!

Although Scott places all of his trades with discretionary wisdom and insight, his fund also uses a highly disciplined risk management approach. For instance, 1 percent is the maximum risk Denali will take on any single trade. The maximum risk allowed in any market sector is 3 percent, and the maximum risk to the portfolio is capped at 10 percent. He also puts strict limits on how much he will allow a profitable trade to retrace.

> Without violating the boundaries of our risk management, however, we use considerable discretion. This discretion enables us to add to or subtract from positions as market conditions warrant—maximizing our potential gain or minimizing our risk. Hence, the average duration of our trades is short. In fact, the majority of our trade exits are discretionary, as a result of changing market conditions and expectations. In essence, our initial stop loss acts as a fail-safe exit strategy if a discretionary exit is not otherwise utilized.

I shared with Scott that his N1 score in trait anxiety is low, which is similar to those of the other great market traders we examined. He replied,

> Well, that makes sense. In order to look for opportunities, you have to be able to be calm and able to think rationally. It is something that I strive for. Nothing is more important during times of market turmoil. When I find myself getting anxious, it is usually because I am in a trade or trades that aren't working. My first reaction is to get out of what isn't working so that I can focus my energy and attention on what is working and the potential opportunity at hand. Basically, I get out first and ask questions later.
>
> I always use stops in my trades. This way I know exactly what my exposure is. Further, if a market looks like it is too volatile or if it isn't behaving the way experience says that it should, I either cut the position entirely, reduce the size, or move the stop. I may get back into the same position the next day, or even the very same day, if the market behaves again as expected. This often results in small losses. I look at it like an insurance policy. I pay a certain premium through small losses in order to protect equity against the big hit.

At first I thought Scott's discussion on anxiety and the markets differed substantially from other traders I interviewed. Other traders had told me that it is important to confront anxiety and not back down when one feels panicky. (Remember the quote from Jerry Rice, too!) So I asked Scott why he flees a position if he is starting to sweat and get nervous. Scott replied:

> It's not that I exit at any moment of uncertainty. It's when the behavior of the market is not what is expected that I get out. For example, if there is a news event and the market is moving against the expected direction, that tells me that the investors are emotional. I don't want to be following the emotions of other investors. I am always gauging the emotions of the market and asking myself, "What is the other guy thinking?" So it's really when there is *anxiety in the market*, and I can feel and sense it myself. That's when I get out of my position and take cover, and I only get back in when I know that the market is behaving how it is supposed to, given the current conditions.
>
> Look, anytime there's money on the line, there will be some anxiety. All of us traders experience anxiety. You *need* to feel it. Eliminating anxiety is not the goal. You need to feel anxiety; it's a great tool. So I really see anxiety as a two-edged sword. It helps you get in tune with what other traders are feeling, but it's also something you are fighting against at the same time, because obviously it is important to stay calm and to think rationally. So it's a balance between not succumbing to your emotions and being able to use them as a barometer of sorts.

I asked Scott if he ever senses performance anxiety as a big-time futures hedge-fund trader.

> Absolutely, it's hard not to when you're managing other people's money and you're in a drawdown. However, it's the path I've chosen, and so I have to deal with it. It is part of the process of trading. So the challenge is to keep things in perspective. I try to break it down into the two issues: first, the anxiety of managing other people's money and, second, the anxiety created by poor performance. I tell clients that if they invest with Denali, I am trading their money exactly as I trade my own. Since I have no control over their decision and they are free to redeem at any month's end, I am able to handle that emotion without issue. As for performance anxiety, I believe that over time, if I am approaching the markets correctly and managing my risk effectively, the drawdown will end and the anxiety will dissipate. I try to focus on the opportunity at hand and not dwell on recent performance.

Scott also had some interesting insights into traders who are overconfident in what they do (he himself rated average on the C1 scale):

> You have to respect the markets. The markets are always right; sometimes I am right with the markets. The minute you start to think you know what's going on is the minute the markets will show you who's really in charge! You must always be respectful of the wisdom of the markets or you will get taught an expensive lesson. In 1980, after a brief period on the floor of the Chicago Mercantile Exchange, I started working as a retail futures broker. I saw some clients who, although they were very smart people, were so overly confident in what they were doing in the markets that they would get ingrained in their beliefs. They wouldn't change their approaches or back down from their beliefs. They wouldn't get out of a losing trade until they were forced to via a margin call, as they never used stops. Anyway, they inevitably lost money because they could not admit that they were wrong. It was a great experience for me. I learned early on that you can't fight the markets or have too much self-confidence. It will destroy you.
>
> And although I do not usually trade impulsively, I have noticed from time to time that it still rears its ugly head. I'm a visual person, and over the years I've seen millions of charts and chart patterns. Occassionally, I'll see a pattern, and I will be compelled to impulsively buy or sell based on the overall picture without knowing much else. Quite frankly, the results are mixed. The best trades occur when I am more patient and formalize a trading plan and then implement the plan as the market reaches my entry and exit targets.

Scott had some interesting commentary on the role of teachers, mentors, and advisors throughout his trading life:

> I never really had a mentor in trading. I am totally self-taught, although I have read my share of books on the subject. As a kid in college I read your dad's books, as well as Wells Wilder's, and it's funny that today I am your dad's next-door neighbor. But anyway, I basically learned to trade in a closet—almost literally. My first office had no windows in it. So I just learned to watch the markets very carefully, and I studied how they related to one another. Now that I live in the Virgin Islands, I feel it's kind of similar in concept. I am far away from the constant chatter of other traders and commentators. It's dangerous to let yourself be

too influenced by others; you have to develop your own style and instincts.

We buy a lot of research at Denali, and I've followed some of the same analysts for years. I have found that they provide value even when they are wrong in their market calls. For example, an analyst might tell me it's a good time to buy gold. If the argument is strong but the price action doesn't validate the argument, then it suggests to me that many others are probably "long and wrong" and will be forced to sell. That creates the opportunity. The point is that whenever you get trade advice from someone else, you should always ask yourself, "Where are they wrong?" And if the market happens to go there, you might have the setup for a great trade the other way!

At this stage in my career I really don't even have to be doing this, trading every day. But I still do. I still really enjoy trading. To me trading is a game, and one I never get tired of playing. I don't care much for Vegas. Gambling is just a process and set of statistical odds. I can sit down at a blackjack table and play, but I never really get into it. I don't have the edge or the time to develop the edge. But the markets are different. There is a lot of satisfaction in going up against the smartest minds and computers and trying to play this very emotional game. Plus, in market trading price-influencing activity is going on around the world and around the clock, and so the complexity of what moves the markets up and down is ever present and endlessly complex.

I like waking up each morning and settling into a new trading day. I enjoy the process, I enjoy the challenge, and I find it to be fun. I am playing a high stakes game every day, and I'm playing to win. I think we all choose our professions based on our motivations and our skills. Fortunately, I chose a business that seems to suit my skill set.

CHAPTER 29

Case Study: "The Perfect Trader"

Let me make it perfectly clear that there is no such thing as "the perfect trader." He or she simply does not exist. People simply can never attain anything close to perfection. All of us have an irrational, emotional component to us that will interfere with our trading. We all make slips and blunders. We all sometimes fail to learn the lessons we are supposed to be learning, and we make the same slips and blunders all over again. That being said, it can still be a useful exercise to summarize the key points of the successful traders' personality traits presented in this book by trying to imagine what the perfect trader would think like, feel like, and act like. If we wanted to build the perfect trader from the ground up, what traits would we instill in him or her?

It turns out that one of the traders who participated in our NEO-AC study—he preferred to remain anonymous, so I will just use his initials (C.M.)—actually scored what might be considered the ideal personality profile for a trader—or at least as near to the ideal as could be hoped for. Based on the accumulated and averaged results of all the successful traders we studied, C.M.'s personality profile nearly matches what we would expect in the perfect trader. (C.M. would be the first to admit that, although he has been a very successful trader for quite a few years, he is still not perfect!)

First, C.M. not only has a very low overall N score, but in particular he has an incredibly low anxiety level (N1 = 2) and an undetectable level of vulnerability (N6 = 0). C.M., based on those numbers, is one cool cucumber when things get dicey

Remember, nearly all of our top traders scored low in both anxiety and vulnerability; this was one of the consistent patterns we saw in our research. C.M. just scores lower than anyone else we tested! Anxiety or fear is the predominant emotion that traders face again and again, so being low in N1 clearly gives someone the upper hand in trading the markets. Under pressure or heat, we would not expect C.M. to easily frazzle or melt down. Staying sharp and mentally focused and not being overcome by anxiety or self-doubt, C.M. is able to spot and crush good setups in the markets when they present themselves.

That's exactly what C.M. tells us he experiences. He has noticed that frequently he has nerves of steel, though he tells us that, of course, there are times that he too becomes anxious. He notes that this is especially the case when the market moves strongly against him over a weekend, when he feels less in control of his trade, and when there are fewer options to manage the situation. He says that anyone is bound to feel anxious at those times and that there is no way to remove anxiety completely from trading.

C.M. feels that what sets him apart from other traders (and I believe this is key, so get your highlighter out!) is that *he does not fear having anxiety.* He does not have anticipatory fear; he does not have anxiety about the possibility of getting weak knees when things get dicey. It is not in the front of his mind. Further, he says that even when an anxious moment does set in, he knows it is going to dissipate quickly. Just by knowing, on a very cognitive level, that he is not going to emotionally fold under pressure is a huge part of C.M.'s success.

Awareness of anxiety, then, sounds very crucial, if we are going to learn from the example of C.M. That may seem like an obvious or even simple point, but it is *huge*! Not only does C.M. not have much anxiety while trading, but he does not have to worry about his emotions controlling him or interfering with what he is trying to do in the markets. He does not have that emotional specter always shadowing him.

Let me use an analogy. It would be like driving down the open desert highway at a very high speed already knowing in advance, with absolute certainty, that there are no highway patrol officers lying in wait for the next 100 miles. Not to advocate speeding on the roads, but with this major fear factor, or obstacle removed, a speeding driver could fly down the highway at a higher rate of speed and—here is the kicker—would be able to do so *more safely* than if he were doing so with he thought "Smokey" might be hiding behind the next billboard. Why? Without the constant thought in the back of his mind that a patrol car could be around the next bend in the road, the speeding driver could put all of his attention into his actual driving technique and any bumps or potholes along the way. He would be more in tune with his car and more apt to pick up on small changes going on in the environment. So too will the trader who is super low in anxiety be able to trade more freely—without constantly having to worry about his emotions and doubts creeping in and taking charge.

On the actions scale (O4) C.M. scores very high. This indicates that C.M. likes to take very big risks, but *not* so much for thrills or excitement. In fact, C.M. reports that all his life he has enjoyed taking various kinds of risks, such as racing motorcycles, catching alligators with his bare hands, and other such activities. "I like a good challenge; it's always been that way. But it's not a competition for me, and it's not because I like to tempt my fortune. It's also not at all important that I prove myself to others or to make people like me. I take risks primarily to prove to myself what I can do. It's all about the personal challenge."

C.M. went on to say that he was especially struck by how clearly the NEO-AC personality test identified this aspect of him. He explained that, although he has been very successful trading the futures markets, his primary motivation for trading is "to tackle a very difficult task, see how hard it really is, and see how well I can do it." This is a very common theme I discovered among the very successful traders. It's not about a thrill or a rush, and not even so much about making lots of money for most of them (although that is always nice); it's really about a sense of mastery or the pursuit of mastery.

On the competence scale C.M. is also very high (C1 = 28), which reflects his self-confidence. His achievement striving is also very high (C4 = 26). A trait commonality shared with the other great traders we tested and interviewed is C.M.'s sheer willpower to be successful. "Tenacity counts for most everything," is the way he puts it. The very best traders, like C.M., have a fierce and uncon-querable determination. They will stop at nothing to be successful. And it shows in their NEO-AC.

C.M. also scored very high on the order facet (C2 = 25). As with other profitable traders high in C2, C.M. uses systems trading a lot. He describes himself as "80 percent a systems trader, 20 percent a discretionary trader." Interestingly, he says that he had to come up with his own set of system rules that work well for him, because he found that "a lot of rules taught in trading courses and books are plain wrong."

C.M. recognizes that the market is always changing and that his systems need to morph along with the market in order to remain relevant. C.M. reports that, in late 2009 after the quantitative easing of the markets, he did not sufficiently adapt his rules and systems to the new market conditions. For the first time as a trader he started losing money, instead of making it, on a consistent basis. It was only after six months of continued losses that he realized what was going on.

Under these new conditions the market was frequently mak-ing consecutive runs of up to a dozen days in a row, or more. The systems and methods he had developed over the years, prior to the quantitative easing, were built to operate on much shorter runs. His systems were no longer valid for the new markets. But it took him a solid half-year to figure out why he was suddenly losing money. His tried and true systems no longer applied to the current market conditions, and yet he was so used to relying on and fol-lowing his systems that he had trouble divorcing himself from the idea that he had to operate by a certain set of rules. Here his high C2 was actually getting the best of him: He was too rigid, unable to bend the rules or make new ones. Only after finally recognizing what was going on and losing a lot of money in the process, did he find a way to adjust his trading methods to the markets' new operating standards. He was then able to resume being a success-ful trader.

A key point here is that those traders who are very high in C, even the very best traders out there, may find themselves getting stuck in their old ways and slow to adapt to changing conditions. Paying close attention to how well we are adapting to new market situations is imperative. Think Darwin and evolution here.

One final thought about our "perfect trader," C.M. While he is clearly not a dummy, it should be pointed out that C.M. never completed high school. Without a high school diploma or any education and training in finance/economics, he has become fabulously successful at something he has a true passion for. This really goes to show that personality and how one manages his or her emotions play a gargantuan-sized role in mastering the markets. Becoming a consistently successful trader has far more to do with the depths of one's determination, the ability to adapt when needed, and being mentally resilient to stressful situations, and far less to do with how educated someone is or maybe even how smart he or she is (IQ).

Mental Edge Tips

When C.M. first started trading the markets years ago, he went broke right off the bat by losing all of the $65,000 he had started with. His failure stemmed from following the trading advice of others. Let me end this chapter with a very instructive mental edge tip and quote from C.M.:

> It was all due to my inexperience and my idiocy. But luckily I had a friend who believed in me and backed me for a second try at the markets. My backer said, "I know you are going to be successful, because you are too stupid to quit trying." Through trial and error, I came to figure things out by myself and developed my own personal trading style that I am comfortable with. That's what it's all about, finding a method that you are comfortable with. Looking back, my initial wipeout was the best thing that ever happened to me, because it forced me to learn to develop my own style instead of just trying to copy someone else's. And I have since learned that those who do well trading the markets right out of the blocks eventually all fail, because they falsely learn and come to believe that trading is not that hard and that anyone can do it. Even later, when they eventually fail, as they all do, they still have this idea that trading isn't that hard of a thing and that they can make money again. They think just by following someone else's model or method they can make money, because they got lucky that first time. I am lucky to have learned the secret to successful trading, and I have had a wonderful run of years because of it.

CHAPTER 30

The Addictive Personality

Speculating in the markets, when practiced the right way, is not gambling. True speculating involves much more than a blind gamble. But on the other hand, there are some people who use Wall Street as a substitute for the Strip in Las Vegas. These traders gamble on the markets—and that kind of market investing can certainly turn into an addiction.

An addiction occurs when a given behavior (food, sex, money, drugs, or what have you) provides an intense stimulation that fuels the brain's reward system. The reward loops and pathways in the brain get so reinforced in the process that the instigating behavior takes on a life of its own. People with addictions seek out the behavior primarily to feed the reward system (to feel good). Oftentimes much of the euphoric effect of the "drug" that was initially enjoyed by the user is eventually depleted or lost, even though the reward center's desire for more and more of the drug persists. Addicts are unable to stop doing the behavior, despite their awareness of substantial negative consequences tied to the behavior.

Successful traders, as we have already seen, want to trade because it is a challenge and a forum to test their mental prowess. It's a true game of chess, one where the stakes are high. Addictive traders, on the other hand, have developed a *need* for trading. Their focus is not on the challenge, but rather on getting a high from the excitement of trading itself. An addicted trader is a poor manager of risk and his money. Addictive traders are unable to stop themselves from trading and hence always overtrade. They feel compelled to keep placing another trade, because they get a rush (a "high") from the actual act of trading. As the intensity and duration of the drug's "high" diminishes, they usually have to use the drug (the trade) on a more frequent basis, and they tend to require larger doses of the drug as well (bigger trades), or turn to drugs with a greater link to excitement (think day trading).

People who are very high in both N and E (a.k.a. "unstable extroverts") are especially prone to adopting addictive behaviors, and particular facets N5 (impulsivity) and E5 (excitement seeking) are involved. People very low in C5 (self-discipline) are also at risk of addictive behaviors. If your personality profile puts you at risk for addictive behaviors or if you have ever wondered whether you may be developing an addiction to trading the markets, it is important that you be screened. Some good screening questions you can ask yourself include:

1. Have I ever tried to cut back on or stop trading only to find that I could not?
2. Has anyone close to me ever told me she is annoyed by how much I trade, or has she even asked me outright to stop trading?
3. Do I ever feel guilty about my trading behaviors?
4. Do I trade simply out of boredom?
5. Am I trading merely to obtain a sense of excitement in my life?
6. Have I developed a pattern in which I am trading larger and larger sums of money in order to achieve the same level of excitement?
7. Have I developed a pattern in which I am trading more frequently, such as having a shorter duration between one trade and the next trade, or where the duration of individual trades is getting shorter?
8. Have my trading losses created problems in my relationships (with my spouse or children)?

9. Have my trading losses caused significant financial problems (borrowing money, selling off personal effects in order to trade, bankruptcy, lien on the house)?
10. Do I find myself preoccupied with trading outside of market hours, at the expense of other important areas in my life (eating healthfully, maintaining the car, and so on)?

If you answered yes to at least three of the above ten questions, it is possible that you have taken on pathological trading behavior and an addiction to trading may be developing. If so, this is serious, and you need to seek a qualified professional assessment (a psychiatrist or a psychologist). Get help right away.

After you get help, *do not* return to trading. Like the alcoholic who relapses because he thinks he will be able to manage or control "just one drink," once your brain has developed a memory of addictive trading behavior, it is forever prewired to lapse right back into it. One drink will surely lead to a full relapse in the alcoholic—and the same thing happens to trading addicts who stubbornly believe they can return to the markets with better self-control the second time around. The social and other environmental cues are too strong. The pathways in the brain have been trained too well. Do not even contemplate the idea of returning to trading if you have a history of a trading addiction.

CHAPTER 31

Conclusions

I hope from reading this book you have learned something about your own personality, both as it pertains to trading the markets and to life in general. Keep in mind that there is no such thing as an "ideal trading personality" that will ensure consistently successful trading. From our personal experience as well as our accumulation of research data on the personalities of some of the world's top traders, we have found that traders with very different personality profiles can certainly succeed, although they generally do share some common traits.

We have uncovered in our studies that although the universe of successful traders is not entirely homogenous, there are some temperamental traits (such as being low in N1 and N6, high in O4 in comparison to E5) which tend to show up more in *populations* of successful traders in comparison to *populations* of general market traders. These particular trait patterns seem to be quite beneficial to trading the markets. It is also true that someone who is conversely very high in N, high in E5, very low in C, and very low in O4 is probably going to really struggle at making a career out of trading the markets. Such a person is prone to impulsively making large and frequent trades, even gambles, and experiences reactive negative emotions, which in turn may interfere with the cognitive tasks needed to execute trading properly.

I hope you have seen and learned that "controlling" or "dampening" your emotions" is *not* the goal of the wise trader. The better approach is *regulating* your emotions. Someone who is very high on the N scale or E scale needs to appreciate that he or she feels emotions strongly and quickly and needs to proactively find ways to compensate for this. But no matter what your scores on the N and E scales, we all have lots of emotions while trading. It is important to recognize that emotions can be both a curse (i.e., they can get in the way of logical thinking) or a blessing (if people can learn to focus and translate some of their emotions into a healthy, competitive drive and determination to succeed).

Meanwhile, traders who are too emotionally stable—low in N— might be able to clearly and rationally use their cerebral cortex without emotional interference, but at the same time they may lack the ability to easily tap into emotions at the appropriate times to spur themselves on (develop a true passion), have an appropriate level of fear or apprehension, and so on. They may be less aware of an oncoming danger or excessive risk because they simply don't have a loud enough emotional fire alarm.

Ultimately your unique personality, which is brought into clearer view using the NEO-AC, is what you have to work with. It is who you are. Personality is what makes someone "someone." It is very difficult to fundamentally change who you are as a person to any significant degree. As an adult your personality is not likely going to change much. If you take the NEO-AC again in 10 or even 20 years, your results will not vary much (unless, of course, you develop Alzheimer's dementia, have a major trauma to the brain, and so forth). Consequently, the key is to fully appreciate the complex melding together of the five factors and thirty facets on the NEO-AC, understand where your personal strengths and weaknesses are, and then learn how to adapt to them through various strategies and techniques.

Do not think of being emotionally stable (low in neuroticism) as being necessarily "better" than being unstable (or neurotic). The key is how far away from average you are and whether or not you can positively adapt to the variations in the excessive trait that you possess. Although our research indicates that low anxiety is a common trait among great traders, this may not be a universal truth, and in fact two of the traders we studied indeed are *not* low on the anxiety scale. These outlier anxiety-prone successful traders have learned—either through personal experience and/or through coaching—how to regulate the emotions that pop up during their trading day.

This same principle, learning to adapt, applies to all of the personality traits. Successful traders are people who are able to bring their personal strengths to bear, meanwhile controlling and mitigating the effects of their personal weaknesses. They align their strengths with the style and method of trading that best suits them, such as using systems versus discretionary trading. They find the right fit between who they are as a person, their overall trading approach or philosophy, and their specific trading methods and plans.

I wish you boundless happiness and personal fulfillment as you travel down the road of knowing yourself better and applying this knowledge to market trading and to other domains in your life as well!

The Personality Facets in Detail

N1: ANXIETY

Very High	Very high scorers are extremely nervous, anxious, tense, and jittery. They are excessively apprehensive and prone to worry, they feel uncertain, and their decisions and actions are often influenced by efforts to avoid danger.
High	High scorers are individuals who are at times apprehensive and fearful. Under stress they especially feel anxious.
Low	Low scorers are calm and relaxed, and they do not dwell on things that could go wrong.
Very Low	Very low scorers lack significant or appropriate feelings of anxiety or apprehension when these feelings are warranted. They fail to expect, anticipate, or appreciate normal, obvious, or readily apparent dangers, risks, threats, or consequences.

N2: ANGRY HOSTILITY

Very High	Very high scorers have episodes of intense and dyscontrolled rage and fury. They are hypersensitive and touchy, easily reacting with anger and hostility toward even minor events, annoyances, or criticisms.
High	High scorers' tendency is to experience anger and related emotional states, such as frustration and bitterness, under stress.

| Low | Low scorers are easygoing and not prone to anger easily. |
| Very Low | Very low scorers suppress appropriate feelings of anger and hostility. They do not even become annoyed or angry when confronted or provoked with substantial abuse, exploitation, harm, or victimization, often to their own detriment. |

N3: DEPRESSION

Very High	These people are continually gloomy and depressed, and they feel hopeless. They feel lonely and lack social support. They tend to have thoughts of feeling worthless, helpless, and excessively guilty. They complain a lot and are self-punitive. They lack satisfaction or meaning in their lives. They may at times feel suicidal.
High	During stressful times, these people are prone to feelings of guilt, sadness, hopelessness, and loneliness. They are easily discouraged and feel dejected during difficult times.
Low	Low scorers are resistant to low moods and feelings of hopelessness under stress.
Very Low	Very low scores indicate a propensity to fail in appreciating actual costs and consequences of losses, setbacks, and failures. They have difficulty in soliciting or maintaining support and sympathy from others after they sustain a loss.

N4: SELF-CONSCIOUSNESS

Very High	Very high scorers are prone to intense feelings of chagrin and embarrassment. They feel mortified, humiliated, ashamed, or disgraced if they make even a small error or omission in the presence of others. Consequently, they avoid social situations and develop poor social skills. They can develop distorted body images, and in severe cases, can feel like imposters, not like their true selves.
High	High scorers are uncomfortable around others, sensitive to ridicule, and prone to feelings of inferiority.
Low	Low scorers are less disturbed by awkward social situations.
Very Low	Very low scorers are indifferent to opinions or reactions of others. They often commit social blunders, insults, or indiscretions because of this indifference. They lack feelings of shame, even for socially egregious acts. They appear glib and superficial.

N5: IMPULSIVENESS

Very High	These people eat or drink to excess and are usually troubled by debts secondary to overspending. They are susceptible to cons, tricks, and poor business and financial decisions. They can rashly engage in a variety of harmful acts, such as binge eating, overuse of drugs, and alcohol or gambling. They are at risk to forms of self-mutilation or even suicide.
High	High scorers have difficulty controlling their cravings and urges, although they may later regret the behavior.
Low	Low scorers find it easier to resist temptations and have a higher tolerance for frustration (not getting what they want).
Very Low	Very low scorers are excessively restrained or restricted. Their lives are dull and uninteresting. They lack spontaneity.

N6: VULNERABILITY

Very High	Very high scorers are overwhelmed by minor stress, and as such, they respond even to minor stressors with panic, helplessness, and dismay.
High	High scorers at times feel unable to cope with stress, frequently becoming dependent, hopeless, or panicked when facing emergency situations.
Low	Low scorers perceive themselves as capable of handling themselves in difficult situations.
Very Low	Very low scorers feel unrealistically invulnerable or invincible to danger. They fail to recognize their own limitations. They fail to take appropriate precautions or obtain necessary support or assistance. They fail to recognize or appreciate signs of illness, failure, or loss.

E1: WARMTH

Very High	Very high scorers develop inappropriate, problematic, or harmful attachments to others. They develop excessive feelings of affection in situations in which formal, neutral, or objective feelings are necessary or preferable. They can be intrusive on others' emotions. They can be sexually seductive or provocative. They are prone to excessive self-disclosure.
High	These people are affectionate and friendly, and they easily form close attachments with others.

| Low | Low scorers are reserved, formal, and distant in manner and hence do not easily form new friendships or attachments. |
| Very Low | These people have severe difficulty developing or sustaining personal, intimate relationships. They are detached, lack personal interest in others, and are indifferent to others' feelings. They have difficulty expressing their own feelings. |

E2: GREGARIOUSNESS

Very High	Very high scorers are unable to tolerate being alone, as they have an excessive need for the presence of others. They place more emphasis on the quantity of relationships (or the need for developing new relationships), rather than on the depth and quality of existing relationships.
High	High scorers enjoy the company of others; the more, the merrier.
Low	Low scorers tend to be loners who do not seek social stimulation.
Very Low	These people are socially isolated. They have no apparent social network, due to social withdrawal.

E3: ASSERTIVENESS

Very High	High scorers are domineering, pushy, bossy, dictatorial, or authoritarian. They always give them, but they refuse to take instructions themselves.
High	High scorers are dominant, forceful, and socially ascendant. They speak without hesitation and often become group leaders.
Low	Low scorers tend to stay in the background and let others do the talking.
Very Low	These people are resigned and ineffectual. They have little influence or authority at work. Also, they have little say in the decisions that affect their own personal lives. They have difficulty expressing wishes and limit-setting with others. They are excessively passive.

E4: ACTIVITY

| Very High | Very high scorers are often overextended, frenzied, frantic, and easily distracted. At times they can burn themselves out. They feel driven to keep busy, filling spare time with numerous and at times trivial or pointless activities, rarely taking time off to relax and recuperate by doing nothing. |
| High | High scorers have a rapid tempo and vigorous movements. They have a sense of energy and need to keep themselves busy. |

| Low | Low scorers are more leisurely and relaxed in tempo, although they are not sluggish or lazy. |
| Very Low | The very low scorers on this facet are inactive, idle, sedentary, and passive. They appear apathetic, inert, and lethargic. |

E5: EXCITEMENT-SEEKING

Very High	These people engage in a variety of reckless and even highly dangerous activities. Their behavior is rash, foolhardy, and careless. They are easily bored by anything less than excessive thrill-seeking.
High	High scorers crave excitement and stimulation.
Low	Low scorers feel little need for thrills and prefer a quiet life that high scorers might find boring.
Very Low	Very low scorers are engaged in activities and apparent pleasures that are habitual, mechanical, and routine. Their lives are experienced as dull, monotonous, and in a rut.

E6: POSITIVE EMOTIONS

Very High	Very high scorers are overly emotional and oftentimes overreact to minor events. They lose control of their emotions during major events. They tend to see life through rose-colored lenses, will often be giddy, and may appear to others to be euphoric or even manic.
High	High scorers laugh easily and laugh often. They are cheerful and optimistic.
Low	Low scorers are less exuberant and high-spirited, though not necessarily unhappy.
Very Low	The very low scorers are severe, austere, solemn, or stern. They appear unable to enjoy themselves at happy events. They remain grim and humorless. They are pessimistic.

O1: FANTASY

Very High	High scorers are often occupied with or distracted by fantasies. Many will confuse reality with fantasy. They may appear to be living in a dream world. They may have "dissociative" or hallucinatory experiences. They are superstitious.
High	High scorers have vivid imaginations and active fantasy lives.
Low	Low scorers are more prosaic and prefer to keep their minds on the task at hand. They keep both feet on the ground.
Very Low	The very low scorers lack any interest in fantasy or daydreams, and their imaginations tend to be sterile. They fail to enjoy activities that involve fantasy or imagination.

O2: AESTHETICS

Very High	These high scorers are preoccupied with aesthetic interests or activities to the detriment of social and occupational functioning. They are driven and obsessed by some form of unusual, peculiar, or aberrant aesthetic activity.
High	High scorers have a deep appreciation for art and beauty. They are moved by poetry, absorbed in music, and intrigued by art.
Low	Low scorers are relatively insensitive to and uninterested in the arts and beauty.
Very Low	Very low scorers have no appreciation for aesthetic or cultural pursuits. They are unable to communicate with or relate to others due to an absence of appreciation for culture or aesthetic interests (for example, artwork "just looks like a bunch of colors to me").

O3: FEELINGS

Very High	These individuals are excessively governed by or preoccupied with their emotions. They may experience the self as continually within an exaggerated mood state and may be excessively sensitive or responsive to transient mood states.
High	High scorers experience deeper and more differentiated emotional states and feel both happiness and unhappiness.
Low	Low scorers have somewhat blunted emotions and do not believe that feeling states are important.
Very Low	Very low scorers are oblivious to the feelings within themselves and within other persons. They may seldom experience substantial or significant feelings. They will appear highly constricted. They are overly rational.

O4: ACTIONS

Very High	The very high scorers are unpredictable in their plans and interests. They may switch careers and jobs numerous times.
High	High scorers prefer novelty and variety to familiarity. These, in general, are the risk-takers.
Low	Low scorers find change and risk difficult. They prefer to stick to the tried and true.
Very Low	These people avoid any change to their daily routines. They establish a set routine in their daily activities and stick to it in a repetitive and habitual manner. They do not have hobbies.

O5: IDEAS

Very High	The very high scorers are preoccupied with unusual, aberrant, or strange ideas. Their reality testing can be tenuous. They can be overly theatrical and abstract.
High	High scorers enjoy both philosophical arguments and brain teasers. They are willing to consider new and unconventional ideas.
Low	Low scorers have limited curiosity and narrowly focus their resources on limited topics.
Very Low	The very low scorers fail to appreciate or recognize new solutions. They reject new, creative, or innovative ideas as strange and "crazy." They repeatedly apply old, failed solutions to new problems. They do better with more straightforward problems and concrete solutions. They are rigidly traditional, old-fashioned, and resistant to new, alternative perspectives or cultures.

O6: VALUES

Very High	Very high scorers continually question and then reject alternative value systems. They lack any clear or coherent guiding belief systems or convictions. They are adrift and lost when faced with moral, ethical, or other significant life decisions. They can be excessively unconventional and permissive.
High	High scorers are ready to reexamine social, political, and religious values.
Low	Low scorers tend to accept authority and honor tradition. They are conservative by nature.
Very Low	Very low scorers are dogmatic and closed-minded with respect to their own moral, ethical, or other belief systems. They reject and are intolerant of alternative belief systems. They may be prejudiced and bigoted. They are overly conventional.

A1: TRUST

Very High	Very high scorers have a tendency to be naive, gullible, and "dewy-eyed." They fail to recognize that some people should not be trusted. They fail to take realistic or practical caution with respect to property, savings, and other things of value.
High	High scorers have a disposition to believe that others are honest and well intentioned.

Low	Low scorers tend to be cynical and skeptical, and they assume that others may be dishonest.
Very Low	Very low scorers are paranoid and suspicious of most people. They readily perceive malevolent intentions in benign, innocent remarks or behaviors. They often are involved in acrimonious arguments with friends, colleagues, associates, or neighbors due to their unfounded beliefs or expectations that they are being mistreated, used, exploited, or victimized.

A2: STRAIGHTFORWARDNESS

Very High	The very high scorers naively and indiscriminately reveal personal secrets, insecurities, and vulnerabilities to other people, thereby exposing themselves to unnecessary exploitation, loss, or victimization. They are unable to be clever, shrewd, cunning, or secretive.
High	High scorers are frank, sincere, and ingenuous.
Low	Low scorers are more willing to manipulate others through flattery, craftiness, or deception.
Very Low	Very low scorers are continually deceptive, dishonest, and manipulative. They con or deceive others for personal profit, gain, or advantage. They likely engage in pathological lying and are themselves unfaithful. Others may quickly or eventually realize that they cannot be trusted.

A3: ALTRUISM

Very High	Very high scorers are excessively selfless and sacrificial. Frequently they are exploited, abused, or victimized due to a failure to consider or be concerned with their own needs or rights.
High	High scorers have an active concern for others' welfare, as shown in their generosity and willingness to step in and assist others in need of help.
Low	Low scorers are somewhat self-centered and are reluctant to get involved in the problems of others.
Very Low	The very low scorers show little regard for the rights of others. They are greedy and stingy. They are exploitive and abusive. They are often envious of others. They are insensitive to others' needs and feelings. They are very self-centered.

A4: COMPLIANCE

Very High	The very high scorers are acquiescent, yielding, docile, and submissive. They are often exploited, abused, or victimized as a result of failure to protect or defend themselves. They have difficulty expressing aggression or anger and lack assertiveness. They are unable to set limits with others.
High	High scorers tend to defer to or cooperate with others. They inhibit aggression or dissent easily. They forgive and forget.
Low	Low scorers are aggressive. They prefer to compete, rather than to cooperate with others. They have no reluctance in expressing their disagreement, even turning to anger if necessary to get their points across.
Very Low	The very low scorers are argumentative, defiant, resistant to authority, contentious, contemptuous, belligerent, combative, or obstructive. They may turn to bullying, intimidating, and even using physical aggression to get what they want. They generally do not get along with others, and they also dislike others. They easily elicit dislike and animosity in others. They are competitive, stubborn, unforgiving, and vengeful.

A5: MODESTY

Very High	The very high scorers are meek and self-denigrating. They fail to appreciate or are unable to acknowledge their talents, abilities, attractiveness, or other positive attributes.
High	High scorers are humble and self-effacing, although they are not lacking in self-confidence or self-esteem.
Low	Low scorers believe they are superior people and may be considered arrogant or conceited by others.
Very Low	The very low scorers are conceited, arrogant, boastful, pretentious, or pompous. They feel entitled to special considerations, treatment, or recognition that they are unlikely to be provided.

A6: TENDER-MINDEDNESS

Very High	The very high scorers are soft-hearted, mawkish, or maudlin. They become excessively depressed, tearful, and overwhelmed in the face of pain and suffering of others. Their feelings of pity and concern are a means for exploitation by others.
High	High scorers are moved by others' needs and emphasize the human side of social policies.

| Low | Low scorers are more hard-headed and less moved by appeals to pity. |
| Very Low | Very low scorers are callous, coldhearted, and at times even merciless and ruthless toward others. They experience no concern, interest, or feelings for the pain and suffering of others. |

C1: COMPETENCE

Very High	Very high scorers seek perfectionism. They may even see themselves as being perfect and are not aware of their shortcomings. They emphasize or value competence in specific areas of their lives, to the detriment of most other activities and interests. They can fail to be successful or even adequate in certain tasks, assignments, and responsibilities due to their excessive perfectionism. They do not enjoy challenges or accomplishments in new areas or disciplines.
High	High scorers feel well-prepared to deal with life. They are capable, sensible, prudent, and effective.
Low	Low scorers have lower opinions of their abilities and admit that they are often unprepared and inept.
Very Low	The very low scorers are lax. They are disinclined, incapable, or unskilled at tasks, despite a potential to be highly, or at least adequately, skilled at those tasks.

C2: ORDER

Very High	The very high scorers are preoccupied with order, rules, schedules, and organization. Their fixation on order undermines leisure activities. Tasks can remain uncompleted due to an overly rigid emphasis upon proper order and organization. Their friends and colleagues grow frustrated by this preoccupation.
High	High scorers are neat, tidy, and well organized. They keep things in their proper places.
Low	Low scorers find it difficult to get organized and describe themselves as unmethodical.
Very Low	The very low scorers are disorganized and sloppy to the point where it can result in haphazard and slipshod work.

C3: DUTIFULNESS

Very High	Very high scorers are so rigidly adherent to a set of rules and standards that they fail to appreciate, acknowledge, or solve ethical and moral dilemmas. They cannot think outside the box. They place duty above all other moral and ethical principles.
High	High scorers adhere strictly to their ethical principles and scrupulously fulfill their moral obligations.
Low	Low scorers are more casual about such matters. They may be somewhat unpredictable and unreliable.
Very Low	Very low scorers are undependable, unreliable, and at times immoral or unethical.

C4: ACHIEVEMENT STRIVING

Very High	The very high scorers are excessively devoted to career, work, or productivity to the detriment of other important areas of life. These are workaholics who sacrifice friends, family, and other relationships for personal achievement or success. They set unrealistically high standards for themselves.
High	High scorers have high aspiration levels and work hard to achieve their goals in life.
Low	Low scorers are lackadaisical and perhaps even lazy. They are not driven to succeed.
Very Low	The very low scorers are aimless, shiftless, and directionless. They have no clear goals, plans, or directions in life. They drift from one job, aspiration, or place to another and never settle down.

C5: SELF-DISCIPLINE

Very High	Very high scorers show single-minded doggedness for trivial, inconsequential, impossible, or even harmful tasks and goals. They cannot disengage from projects or set aside incomplete jobs once they have started, even when it is imperative that they do so.
High	High scorers have the ability to motivate themselves to get the job done.

| Low | Low scorers procrastinate in beginning a given task, and once they begin, they are easily discouraged and eager to quit before completing the job at hand. |
| Very Low | Very low scorers are notable for employment that is unstable and marginal. They are negligent at work and do not finish tasks. They are excessively hedonistic and self-indulgent. They have difficulty concentrating and maintaining their attention. They have troubles budgeting money. They have poor health habits. They are unable to change maladaptive behaviors and often show unrestricted use of alcohol, nicotine, or other drugs. |

C6: DELIBERATION

Very High	The very high scorers are prone to ruminations or excessive pondering of all possible consequences to the point that decisions fail to be made on time, effectively, or at all.
High	High scorers are cautious and deliberate. They think carefully before acting or speaking out.
Low	Low scorers are hasty and often speak or act without considering the consequences.
Very Low	Very low scorers are hasty and careless in their decision making, even to the point of sustaining harmful or dire consequences. They fail to consider various consequences and costs, even in important life decisions.

The Styles of Personality

STYLE OF WELL-BEING

E–, N+ Gloomy Pessimists	E+, N+ Overly Emotional
These people face a dark and dreary life. There can be little that cheers them and much in life that causes them anguish and distress. Especially under stressful circumstances, they may succumb to periods of clinical depression, and even when they are functioning normally they can still find life hard and joyless.	These people experience both positive and negative emotions fully and may swing rapidly from one mood to another. Their interpersonal interactions may be tumultuous because they are so easily carried away by their feelings. They may show features of histrionic personality disorder, but they may also feel that their lives are full of excitement. These people are at high risk for substance abuse disorders.
E–, N– Low-Keyed	E+, N– Upbeat Optimists
Neither good news nor bad has much effect on these people. They maintain a stoic indifference to events that would either frighten or delight others. Their interpersonal relationships may suffer because other people find them to be "cold fish." Their emotional experience of life is bland.	These people are usually cheerful, because they are not unduly troubled by problems, and they have a keen appreciation of life's pleasures. When faced with frustration or disappointment, they may become angry or sad more easily than others, but then quickly put those feelings behind them. They prefer to concentrate on the future, which they view with eager anticipation. They enjoy life.

STYLE OF DEFENSE

(O–, N+) **Maladaptive**	(O+, N+) **Hypersensitive**
These individuals tend to use primitive and ineffective defenses, such as repression, denial, and reaction formation. They prefer not to think about disturbing ideas, and they may refuse to acknowledge possible dangers (such as serious illness). They lack insight into the distressing feelings that they experience, and because they can not verbalize their feelings, they may be considered alexithymic.	Hypersensitive people seem undefended. They are alert to danger and vividly imagine possible misfortunes. They may be prone to nightmares. Because they think in unusual and creative ways, they may sometimes be troubled by odd and eccentric ideas.
(O–, N–) **Hyposensitive**	(O+, N–) **Adaptive**
Hyposensitive individuals rarely experience strong negative emotions, and when they do, they downplay their importance. They do not dwell on threats or losses, turning instead to concrete actions to solve the problem at hand or simply to distract themselves. They put their faith in higher powers.	Adaptive individuals are keenly aware of conflict, stress, and threats and are able to utilize these situations to stimulate creative adaptations. They grapple intellectually with their own intrapsychic problems, and they tend to react to life stressors with humor and artistic inspiration.

STYLE OF INTERESTS

(O–, E+) **Mainstream Consumers**	(O+, E+) **Creative Interactors**
Their interests reflect the popular favorites: parties, sports, music, blockbuster movies, shopping, and other such events where they can enjoy themselves with others. They are attracted to jobs or careers that let them work with others on simple projects. Possible vocation: salesperson.	These individuals' interests revolve around the new and the different. They like to share their discoveries with others. They enjoy public speaking, and they fit in well in discussion groups. They enjoy meeting people from different backgrounds. Possible vocations: teacher or anthropologist.
(O–, E–) **Homebodies**	(O+, E–) **Introspectors**
Their interests are focused on activities they can pursue alone or with a small group. They are unadventurous and likely hobbies include collecting items like stamps or coins, gardening, and watching TV. Their vocational interests may include mechanical or domestic work. Possible vocation: bookkeeper.	Their interests are focused on ideas and activities they can pursue alone. Reading, writing, or creative hobbies such as painting and music appeal to them. They prefer occupations that provide both challenge and privacy. Possible vocations: artist, naturalist.

STYLE OF ANGER CONTROL

(A–, N+) Temperamental	(A+, N+) Timid
Temperamental people are easily angered and tend to express anger directly. They may fly into a rage over a minor irritant, and they can seethe with anger for long periods of time. They are deeply involved in themselves and take offense readily, and they often overlook the effects of their anger on others. They also may be prone to physical aggression or verbal abuse.	Timid people are heavily conflicted over anger. On the one hand, their feelings are readily hurt, and they often feel victimized. On the other hand, they are reluctant to express anger because they do not want to offend others. Their anger may be directed inwardly toward themselves.
(A–, N–) Cold-Blooded	(A+, N–) Easy-Going
Cold-blooded people "don't get mad; they get even." These people often take offense, but they are not overpowered by feelings of anger. Instead, they keep accounts and express their animosity at a time and in a way that suits them. They may seek revenge in criminal assaults, or more commonly, in manipulative office politics or exploitive interpersonal relationships.	Easy-going people are slow to anger and are reluctant to express their anger when it arises. They know when they have been insulted and may raise objections, but they would prefer to forget and forgive. They understand that there are two sides to every issue, and they try to work toward a common ground in resolving disputes.

STYLE OF IMPULSE CONTROL

(C–, N+) **Undercontrolled**	(C+, N+) **Overcontrolled**
These individuals are often at the mercy of their own impulses. They find it difficult and distressing to resist any urge or desire, and they lack the self-control to hold their urges in check. As a result, they may act in ways that they know are not in their long-term best interests. They may be particularly susceptible to substance abuse and other health-risk behaviors.	These people combine distress-proneness with a strong need to control their behavior. They have perfectionistic strivings and will not allow themselves to fail, even at the smallest detail. Because their goals are often unrealistic, they are prone to guilt and self-recrimination. They may be susceptible to obsessive and compulsive behavior.
(N–, C–) **Relaxed**	(C+, N–) **Directed**
These people see little need to exert rigorous control over their behavior. They learn to take the easy way, and they are philosophical about disappointments. They may need extra assistance in motivating themselves to follow appropriate medical advice or to undertake any effortful endeavor.	These people have a clear sense of their own goals and the ability to work toward them, even under unfavorable conditions. They take setbacks and frustration in stride, and they are able to tolerate unsatisfied needs without abandoning their plans of action.

STYLE OF INTERACTIONS

(A−, E+) Leaders	(A+, E+) Welcomers
These people enjoy social situations as an arena in which they can shine. They prefer giving orders to taking them and believe they are particularly well suited to making decisions. They may be boastful and vain, but they also know how to get people to work together.	These people sincerely enjoy the company of others. They are deeply attached to their old friends and reach out freely to new ones. They are good-natured and sympathetic, willing to lend an ear, and happy to chat about their own ideas. They are easy to get along with and popular.
(A−, E−) Competitors	(A+, E−) The Unassuming
These people tend to view others as potential enemies. They are wary and distant and keep to themselves. They prefer respect to friendship and guard their privacy jealously. When interacting with them, it is wise to allow them the space they feel they need.	These people are modest and self-effacing. They often prefer to be alone, but they are also sympathetic and respond to others' needs. Because they are trusting, others may sometimes take advantage of them. Their friends should watch out for their interests, but still respect their privacy.

STYLE OF ACTIVITY

(C−, E+) Fun-Lovers	(C+, E+) Go-Getters
They are full of energy and vitality, but they find it hard to channel their energy in constructive directions. Instead, they prefer to enjoy life with thrills, adventures, and raucous parties. They are spontaneous and impulsive, ready to drop work for the chance to have a good time.	They are productive and efficient and work at a rapid tempo. They know exactly what needs to be done and are eager to pitch in. They might design their own self-improvement programs and follow them with zeal. They may seem pushy if they try to impose their style on others.
(C−, E−) The Lethargic	(C+, E−) Plodders
They are unenthusiastic and have few plans or goals to motivate them. They tend to be passive and respond only to the most pressing of demands. They rarely initiate activities, and in group activities or games they often find themselves left behind.	They are methodical workers who concentrate on the task at hand. They work slowly and steadily until the job is completed. In leisure as in work, they have a measured pace. They cannot be hurried, but they can be counted upon to finish whatever tasks they are assigned.

STYLE OF ATTITUDES

(A–, O+) **Free-Thinkers**	(A+, O+) **Progressives**
They are critical thinkers who are not swayed by either tradition or sentimentality. They consider all views, but then make their own judgments about right and wrong, and they are willing to disregard others' feelings in pursing their own ideas of the truth.	They take a thoughtful approach to social problems and are willing to try new solutions. They have faith in human nature and are confident that society can be improved through education, innovation, and cooperation. They believe in reason and being reasonable.
(A–, O–) **Resolute Believers**	(A+, O–) **Traditionalists**
These individuals have strong and unchanging beliefs about social policies and personal morality. Because they view human nature with considerable skepticism, they support strict discipline and a get-tough approach to social problems. They expect everyone to follow the rules.	These individuals rely on the beliefs and values of their families and heritages in seeking the best way for people to live. They feel that following the established rules without question is the best way to ensure peace and prosperity for everyone.

STYLE OF LEARNING

(C–, O+) Dreamers	(C+, O+) Good Students
They are attracted to new ideas and can develop imaginative elaborations, but they may get lost in flights of fancy. They are good at starting innovative projects, but they are less successful in completing them and may need help in staying focused. They are able to tolerate uncertainty and ambiguity.	Although they are not necessarily more intelligent than others, these people combine a real love of learning with the diligence and the organization to excel. They have a high aspiration level and are often creative in their approaches to solving problems. They are likely to go as far academically as their gifts (intellectual capacity) will allow.
(C–, O–) Reluctant Scholars	(C+, O–) By-the-Bookers
Academic and intellectual pursuits are not their strength or preference. They need special incentives to start learning and stick with it. They may need help in organizing their work and reminders to keep them on schedule. They may have problems maintaining attention.	These individuals are diligent, methodical, and organized, and they abide by all the rules. However, they lack imagination and prefer step-by-step instructions. They excel at rote learning but have difficulties with questions that have no one right answer. They have a need for structure and closure.

STYLE OF CHARACTER

(C–, A+) **Well-Intentioned**	(C+, A+) **Effective Altruists**
They are giving, sympathetic, and genuinely concerned about others. However, their lack of organization and persistence means that they sometimes fail to follow through on their good intentions. They can be very adept at inspiring kindness and generosity in others.	These are people who work diligently for the benefit of the group. They are high in self-discipline and endurance, and they channel their efforts to the service of others. As volunteers, they are willing to take on difficult or thankless tasks and will stick with them until they get the job done.
(C–, A–) **Undistinguished**	(C+, A–) **Self-Promoters**
They are more concerned with their own comfort and pleasure than with the well being of others. They tend to be weak-willed and are likely to have some undesirable habits they find difficult to correct.	These people are concerned first and foremost with their own needs and interests, and they are effective in pursuing their own ends. They may be highly successful in owning their own businesses or in politics because of their single-minded pursuit of their own interests.

NOTES

Chapter 3
1. G. Soros. *Soros on Soros: Staying Ahead of the Curve*. New York: John Wiley, 1995.
2. M. Gladwell. *Blink: The Power of Thinking Without Thinking*. Boston: Little Brown/Back Bay Books, 2005.
3. M. LeGault. *Think: Why Crucial Decisions Can't Be Made in the Blink of an Eye*. New York: Simon and Schuster, 2006.

Chapter 4
1. P. McHugh and P. Slavney. *The Perspectives of Psychiatry*, second edition, Baltimore: Johns Hopkins University Press, 1998.

Chapter 6
1. T. Canli, et al. "Amygdala Response to Happy Faces as a Function of Extraversion." *Science* June 21, 2002: 2191.

Chapter 14
1. A. Lo, D. Repin, and B. Steenbarger. "Fear and Greed in Financial Markets: A Clinical Study of Day-Traders." *Cognitive Neurosciences Foundations of Economic Behaviors* (2005) 72/2: 287–312.
2. R. Peterson et al. "The Personality Traits of Successful Investors During the U.S. Stock Market's 'Lost Decade' of 2000–2010." Market Psych LLC report, n.d. Unpublished white paper.

Chapter 15
1. B. Knutson et al. "Selective Alteration of Personality and Social Behavior by Serotonergic Intervention, *American Journal of Psychiatry* 155/3: 373–379.
2. A. Jorm. "Modifiability of Trait Anxiety and Neuroticism: A Meta-Analysis of the Literature, *Australian and New Zealand Journal of Psychiatry* (1989) 23: 21–29.
3. T. Tang et al. "Personality Change During Depression Treatment," *Archives of General Psychiatry* (2009) 66/12: 1322–1330.
4. K. Glinski and A. Page. "Modifiability of Neuroticism, Extraversion, and Agreeableness by Group Cognitive Behavior Therapy for Social Anxiety Disorder," *Behavior Change* (2010) 27/1: 42–52.

Chapter 16

1. C. Mayfield et al. "Investment Management and Personality Type," *Financial Review Services* (2008) 17: 219–236.
2. N. Nicholson et al. "Personality and Domain-Specific Risk Taking," *Journal of Risk Research* (2005) 8/2: 157–176.
3. D. Knoch et al. "Disruption of Right Prefrontal Cortex by Low-Frequency Repetitive Transcranial Magnetic Stimulation Induces Risk-Taking Behavior," *Journal of Neuroscience* (2006) 26/24: 6469–6472.
4. D. Smith and R. Whitelaw. "Time-Varying Risk Aversion and the Risk Return Relation" (June 19, 2009), 23rd Australasian Finance and Banking Conference, 2010 paper.

Chapter 17

1. A. Lo, D. Repin, and B. Steenbarger. "Fear and Greed in Financial Markets: A Clinical Study of Day-Traders." *Cognitive Neurosciences Foundations of Economic Behavors* (2005) 95/2: 352–359.
2. T. Odean. "Do Investors Trade Too Much?" *American Economic Review* (December 1999) 89: 1279–1298.
3. B. Biais et al. "Judgmental Overconfidence, Self-Monitoring, and Trading Performance in an Experimental Financial Market." *Review of Economic Studies* (2005) 72/2: 287–312.

Chapter 20

1. P. Costa and R. McRea. "Influence of Extraversion and Neuroticism on Subjective Well-Being: Happy and Unhappy People. *Journal of Personality and Social Psychology* (1980) 38/4: 668–678.

Chapter 22

1. L. Williams. *Confessions of a Radical Tax Protestor.* Hoboken, NJ: John Wiley, 2011.

Chapter 24

1. K. Angle. *One Hundred Million Dollars in Profits: An Anatomy of a Market Killing.* Bay Shore, NY: Windsor Books, 1989.

Chapter 27

1. R. Vince. *Risk Opportunity Analysis.* Amazon's CreateSpace Independent Publishing Platform, 2012.
2. E. Thorp. *Beat the Dealer.* New York: Random House/Vintage Books, 1962. Revised edition, 1966.
3. R. Vince. *Portfolio Management Formulas.* New York: John Wiley, 1990.

INDEX

DR. JASON WILLIAMS is a Johns Hopkins Hospital–trained psychiatrist. He has subspecialty training in psychosomatic medicine and was taught how to use and interpret the world's foremost personality test, the NEO PI-RTM, by one of the co-inventors of the tool. Dr. Williams lives in northern Virginia and practices both inpatient and outpatient psychiatry there. Some of his patients/clients are high-net-worth individuals who seek to maximize their wealth through better mental health.

Larry Williams is a full-time trader and fund manager who speaks at major investment conferences throughout the world. He has created numerous market indicators, including the Williams % R, the Ultimate Oscillator, COT indicators, and the POIVI (Price Open Interest Volume Accumulation Indicator). He is currently on the board of directors for the National Futures Association, which represents commodity trading advisors. Larry Williams has written seven books on stocks and trading.